Walnut Wine
& Truffle Groves

Walnut Wine
& Truffle Groves

Culinary Adventures in the Dordogne

France's Best-Kept Culinary Secret

BY KIMBERLEY LOVATO
RECIPES BY CHEF LAURA SCHMALHORST
PHOTOS BY LOU LESKO

RUNNING PRESS
PHILADELPHIA · LONDON

9 8 7 6 5 4 3 2 1
Digit on the right indicates the number of this printing

Library of Congress Control Number: 2009935549
ISBN 978-0-7624-3799-3

Cover and interior design by Jason Kayser
Typography: Adobe Garamond, Copperplate, and Hadriano

Running Press Book Publishers
2300 Chestnut Street
Philadelphia, PA 19103-4371

Visit us on the web!
www.runningpresscooks.com

Photo on front cover (top) ©iStockphoto.com/compassandcamera

Photos on pages 30, 43, 67, 71, 79, 114, 115, 125, 134, 138, 142, 145, 154 (right), 191, 205, 209, 210, 216, 219 by Kimberley Lovato

Photo on page 23 (top left) courtesy of Louise and Damien Bartlett

Photos on pages 52 (top photos), 147, 160, 168 (bottom photos), 171 (right), 173 (top) by Wilna Wilkinson

Photos on pages 92, 95, 184, 187, 189 by Peter Swiatek

Photos on pages 109 and 120 courtesy of Eric Vidal

Photos on pages 166 and 172 by Ken Cooper

Photo on page 168 (top) by Roland Manouvrier

Photo on page 62 "Chicken Grilling On Rotisserie" ©iStockphoto.com/KSG Designs

Photo on page 96 "To Collect Mushrooms" ©iStockphoto.com/Typo-graphics

Photo on page 141 "Chanterelles In A Basket" ©iStockphoto.com/George Jurasek

Photo on page 165 "Strawberry Time" ©iStockphoto.com/Craetive

To my husband John and daughter, Chloe, for their support and inspiration, and to the people of the Dordogne, for sharing their tables with me.

TABLE OF CONTENTS

"Quel est le plaisir
d'un secret quand on
ne peut pas le partager?"

("What's the fun of a secret
if we can't share it?")

ACKNOWLEDGEMENTS

It is difficult to put into words the gratitude for those who have helped produce this book. We can't single everyone out but we must say thank you to a vital few. To Sally Ann, whose support and friendship is a treasured souvenir; To Roland, whose stories about his beloved Périgord and its history have made us love the place even more; To Wilna whose passion and generosity are infectious; To our families and friends, who stood by us and never stopped believing in our dream of seeing this book on the shelves. Finally, we must thank the warm and hospitable people of the Dordogne for opening their hearts and homes to share their recipes and stories with us. This book has been a labor of love in all respects and we know when the final page turns, it will not the end but rather a beginning of a lifetime of great friendships and meals from the Dordogne.

Kimberley Lovato and Laura Scmalhorst

Foreword

◄◆►

IN spring 2007, I received an e-mail asking me whether I would agree to meet two young women who were eager to write a book on the Périgord, my home. The book as I understood it was to be a travel guide and tribute to Périgourdine life and gastronomy, of which I am so proud. I accepted and, I must say, promptly forgot. But Laura and Kimberley are quite tenacious, and it wasn't long before I received a slew of e-mails proposing dates and times for a meeting.

It should be known that a key characteristic of living Périgourdine and even of the culinary customs is people's casual attitude toward time, and perhaps more important, their willingness to *take* the time to live and enjoy all that the region has to offer. To some extent even forgetting time and its constraints and just letting oneself go is the real rhythm of the region. So even though it annoyed me somewhat that Laura and Kimberley were so strict with their time, they were also very serious about their work, which for me was a favorable point. When I spoke with Kimberley on the phone, her voice was compelling to me, so I agreed to a visit on a day that I had also invited a California journalist and his family to my home at the Borderie, to thank him for hosting me on his radio show.

Laura and Kimberley, along with their photographer, Lou, arrived on time and decided to quickly jump into questions and answers. What struck me was how intelligent, qualified, and passionately interested they were in my culture and the cuisine of the Périgord. Kimberley was eager to know everything, and I asked them to stay a while longer, promising that we'd get to all the questions in time. It was a very pleasant moment for me, answering their questions while preparing lunch for my guests. In the Périgord, one does not let visitors leave at mealtime, so when my guests arrived, I quickly added three additional plates to the table, and Kimberley, Laura, and Lou accepted my invitation to sit down and spend an afternoon around my table. Time slipped by, and all work was forgotten to enjoy this meal among friends.

It was one of those summer days when life was beautiful. There was sun, but not too much. The birds were singing, but not too loudly. The air was soft, but just enough to comfort us. And the company? Ah, the company!

Humor, good moods, laughter, exchanges of culture and, of course, hearty appetites. We spent one exquisite day around my table, and while I know well that I did not answer all of Kimberley's questions, I am most certain that by the end of that day, she and her friends knew the Dordogne and its treasures.

After spending that time with them, I know that this book will be a success. I am honored to be a part of it and am impatient to read it myself. Thank you, Kimberley and Laura, for taking the time to visit—and to understand the beauty and wonder of the Périgord.

Return to see me again soon.

Daniele Mazet-Delpeuch

Chasing Fairy Tales

❖

DREAMS are often born in the most unsuspecting places. Mine happened to be delivered by the postman. The postcard that arrived nearly sixteen years ago depicted the most beautiful village I had ever seen. Nicole and Claude, a couple my husband, Steve, and I had met outside of Paris the year before, sent it to tempt us to explore further in their native France. The picturesque village was enveloped in fog and huddled against a cliff at the edge of the Dordogne River with a dilapidated boat tied to its shore. On the back of the card, in small, black print, were the words "La Roque-Gageac, Dordogne." I tacked the postcard on my kitchen wall amid family pictures and to-do lists and vowed we would find this place one day.

Steve and I have been traveling to the Dordogne for over fifteen years now. With books, maps, magnifying glass, and a positive attitude, we have scoured the region from top to bottom, inside out. Along our aimless path we discovered a land of unspoiled beauty that has spoiled us rotten. Nothing can replicate the awe of seeing for the first time a five-hundred-year-old castle looming over the Dordogne River; neither could I be more inspired than by five generations of family working side by side on their ancestral winery. Every nook and cranny of the Dordogne revealed diverse landscapes and regional history. We passed scene after scene of farmlands with vast fields of corn, sunflowers, and trees dripping with cherries, walnuts, and plums; mountains and rolling hills; dense forests and open meadows; storybook villages and immense châteaux. Our camera was put into overdrive, but our pictures could never quite capture the essence of what we saw. How do you photograph the footsteps of prehistoric man, the grottoes, and the cliffside caves

where traces of humanity date back five hundred thousand years? The fortified towns, called *bastides*, heavily concentrated in the Dordogne, intrigued, as did other medieval villages, like Sarlat, which rest preserved in time. The more than one thousand castles of the region range from Renaissance opulence to feudal fortresses built during eras ravaged by war, of which there have been many in the Dordogne. Even the smallest hamlets revealed memorials to those who gave their lives during past conflicts.

While we easily succumbed to the fairy-tale scenery, we soon realized it was merely a two-dimensional facade without the personalities behind the ancient doors. After years of frequenting the same hotels, restaurants, farms, shops, and daily markets, Steve and I slowly got to know the families, and we were invited into their homes and kitchens. From those with deeply seeded roots in the Périgord to those planting new foreign life in the region, there is a common thread among them—passion. Sitting down at the table with these bon vivants revealed more in one dinner than all the wrinkled maps and glossy guidebooks ever told me. I found the people of the Dordogne delightful and eager to share their stories and secrets. It was here at the table that our story really began.

When Steve and I first officially launched our culinary tour company in 2003, the Dordogne was a natural choice for us. A writer from a local magazine was sent along to cover the events of our inaugural journey. This writer, Kimberley Lovato, had insatiable wanderlust and possessed a zeal for France, its people, its good food, and most important, a gift for imploring others to feel as passionately as she did. Over the years, she has joined us on many of our culinary voyages and traveled with us around Europe, meeting our friends and sharing in our memories. Like us, Kimberley fell instantly in love with the Dordogne. She conceived the idea for this book, and we eagerly signed on. As an added bonus, she speaks French and lives full-time in Europe, which helped push us along a little faster. Little did we know our meeting all those years ago in a small village in the Dordogne would be the preamble to such a great journey.

Kimberley conducted most of our interviews in French (or at least she tried her best). A smile accompanied by a genuine hello (*bonjour*), please (*s'il vous plait*), and thank you (*merci*) go a long way in any language, and her willingness to speak French uncovered a reciprocal graciousness and desire to be understood. Nothing surprised us more than meeting a truffle farmer in the middle of nowhere who spoke to us enthusiastically in perfect English. We had more communication difficulties in our own car with me trying to say *juillet* (July), pronounced jwee-ay in French, but instead saying joo-lee-et, as in Romeo and Juliet. Kimberley, looking confused as she flipped through our packed agenda, finally asked, "Who is Juliet? She is not on our agenda today." We needed a translator from backseat English to front-seat English.

Like language, food is culturally significant in France. Days are planned around meals, shops are closed from noon to 2 p.m. for lunch, and expressions related to food are pervasive. During the research for our book, Kimberley and I documented a few of our favorites, but perhaps the one that resonated the most was "*Vous avez du pain sur la planche,*" (you have some bread on the plank) meaning, "You have your work cut out for you." The Dordogne is world famous for its cuisine, thanks to truffles and foie gras, and traditional cooking is the best glimpse into a culture and culinary history steeped, quite literally, in duck fat. We ate potatoes, *cèpes* (porcini mushrooms), and omelettes all cooked in this magic elixir, which is a staple in the Périgord pantry. We enjoyed locally grown products and the prolific ovens at the affordable and traditional *fermes auberges* (farmhouse inns) that flourish in the Dordogne and offer a glimpse into regional cooking. There are also four Michelin-star restaurants in the region, and two more in nearby

Lot-et-Garonne, confirming that Périgord cuisine is reaching new heights of appreciation. Surprising to us was the amount of seafood and international cuisine making its way onto restaurant menus. Fish and eel pulled from the Dordogne River and scallops and mussels from the seaside were an unexpected addition to many of the menus, and the blending of Asian and African spices with local products tempted our taste buds. The region's menus

are not all duck, contrary to popular misconceptions. Game, beef, lamb, and hearty stews combine with the fresh produce of the region to make eating a more enjoyable experience replete with choice.

Cooking and dining is the glue of social life in the Dordogne, and as we bounced (or perhaps rolled) from table to table, we imagined the decades of decisions, arguments, trysts, and revelations that transpired inside these French kitchens. Recipes, we realized, are as cherished an heirloom as old photos and wedding china. They are passed down (rarely, if ever, on paper) between generations, subtly refined according to new tastes and traditions, but at the core remains fresh local products and a rich pedigree.

Together Kimberley and I invite you to loosen your belt buckles and join us on our edible journey down roads less traveled and into the homes and hearts of some remarkable people. Pull up a chair as we venture down the back roads to navigate the menus and markets with an insatiable appetite for discovery, and a fork and knife at the ready! Through these tales from the table, recipes, and photos, the best of the Dordogne will reveal itself to be more than just a glossy picture on the front of a postcard, but also a living and breathing tapestry woven with the thread of tradition and the colorful dye of eclectic people.

By the way, Steve and I found the image on the postcard that tempted us all those years ago. We were driving along the D703, when suddenly there it was, in black and white: a sign that read La Roque-Gageac. Right before us, the fairy-tale village hewn was real, and there was even a worn rowboat slapping against the shore. We knew then we had found a very special place. After all these years, our own postcard has become creased and yellowed with age, yet the image before us was untouched by time.

Enjoy the journey and bon appétit!

Chef Laura Schmalhorst

Introduction

❖ ◆ ❖

ALL of our favorite things about travel can be found in the Dordogne: great food, fine wine, welcoming people, historic sites, quaint villages, and fairy-tale scenery. The Dordogne has something for any traveler and any lover of the good things in life. Located in the southwestern part of the country, one hundred miles east of Bordeaux, the Dordogne is also known as Périgord. These monikers are synonymous when referring to the region and are used interchangeably, but the cuisine and the recipes are referred to as Périgourdine. Until the eighteenth century the entire region was called Périgord, but in 1790, when the departments of France were created, many took the names of rivers found within the territory. The Dordogne is further divided into (and often referred to by) four colored regions:

> *Périgord Vert* (Green Périgord) is characterized by lush valleys and forests.
>
> *Périgord Blanc* (White Périgord) is so called because of the vast deposits of limestone there.
>
> *Périgord Poupre* (Purple Périgord) derives its name from the grapevines around the Bergerac region.
>
> And finally, *Périgord Noir* (Black Périgord) refers to the region's abundant dense, dark forests of oak trees.

◀ Even one-way roads did not deter us.

The Dordogne is easily accessible by train, plane, and automobile. We should know—we have driven in, flown in, high-speed trained in, hot air ballooned over, and canoed around the Dordogne. As remarkably easy as it is to get here, the Dordogne is relatively less trod upon than other parts of France, giving it an undiscovered and unblemished appeal. No doubt July and August have their share of clogged intersections and parking problems, but compared to Provence or the Côte d'Azur during the same period, the Dordogne is undiscovered territory. Once in the region, a car is essential. The two-lane roads are well marked, but signs can be miniscule, especially the hand-painted ones directing you to local farms, or marked with single words like *miel* (honey). Be warned: some signs lure you around like Hansel and Gretel's breadcrumbs, only to completely disappear altogether. It didn't take long to adjust to getting lost, and we learned to regard it as part of the adventure. In fact, it was on a quest for a walnut farm (which we never found) that we discovered the unfinished *bastide* of Molières, a decidedly undeveloped village that is eerily empty at all times of the day, any day, and gives the impression of being unchanged by time.

The Dordogne

FRANCE

Augignac
Nontron
La Coquille
Bandiat
Dronne
Côle
Thiviers
Brantôme
Sorges
Bourdeilles
Lizonne
Isle
Auvézère
Bertric-Burée
Dronne
Hautefort
Ribérac
Cubjac
Saint-Aulaye
Périgeux
Saint Astier
Thenon
Douzillac
Isle
Vergt
Mussidan
Vézère
Saint-Geniés
Le Bugue
Trémolat
Sarlat-a-Canéda
Vélines
La Force
Creysse
Saint-Cyprien
Dordogne
Bergerac
Lalinde
Gardonne
Dordogne
Cadouin
Domme
Monbazillac
Beaumont
Belvés
Sigoulés
Daglan
Issigeac
Monpazier
Biron

N

0   5   10   15   20 km

It is crucial to recognize that time takes a respite in the Dordogne. On one of our first visits someone asked us, "When you live in a fairy tale, is there any reason to rush?" Point taken. And so we stopped. Once you adjust your attitude to this way of thinking, things get a whole lot easier. We learned many things over our years of visiting, and some of the more important "time" lessons we pass on to you: A delay in taking an order or honoring an appointment to the minute (or hour) is not a personal slam against your nationality. It is simply the way it is. Never plan a meeting on a Sunday. Sundays in France are sacred and reserved for the market, family, church, and the cherished midday meal. The phrase "quick bite" does not exist, and no matter when you arrive at a restaurant, or how many times you clink the silverware together or sigh in frustration, you will leave two hours later, just like everyone else. Face it: France is a slow food nation and most meals, even simple ones, are carefully prepared and meant to be relished, not served in a cardboard box from a clown's mouth and eaten on the road. For those used to schedules, we offer these helpful translations:

> It's only 20 minutes away. = It's 40 minutes away.
>
> Get to the market early. = Get to the market before 7:30 a.m. if you hope to actually see and touch any food.
>
> We'll arrive at 10 a.m. = We will arrive sometime after 10 a.m.
>
> We're in a hurry. = Sorry, there is no translation.

We promise—this slowdown in attitude and newfound flexibility in your agenda will allow you to savor the scenery and meals a little longer, and you'll soon discover what all the fuss is about.

THE FRENCH TABLE

In French households, friends and family are often invited for a Sunday meal, usually at midday, which will last three to four hours. A traditional French lunch or dinner always includes three courses: an appetizer, a main course, and a dessert. However, dining in France is a national sport, and thus the meal could last two to four hours and may include these additional courses:

APÉRITIF

This is a small sip of liquor, sweet wine, or even champagne on special occasions. *Vin de noix* [walnut wine] is a typical choice in the Dordogne, as is a sweet Monbazillac wine, often served with foie gras. Apéritifs are offered before taking your order in a restaurant, and if invited to a private home, it's customary to have an apéritif about thirty minutes before sitting down to the meal.

AMUSE-BOUCHE

The word in French literally translates to "mouth amuser." An amuse-bouche is a tiny teaser served before the entrée and often accompanied by an apéritif. It could be anything from pâté and bread to fruit or vegetables.

L'ENTRÉE

Meaning "appetizer" in French, this course could be an assortment of hot or cold foods such as charcuterie, a soup, or even a small salad. Unlike in the United States, items listed under the heading "*Les Entrées*" in France are not the main course.

LE PLAT PRINCIPAL

The main course is usually meat served with a side dish of vegetables. In the Dordogne, duck confit [duck leg] or *magret* [duck breast] are common, but lamb, beef, game, and fish are served as well. Side dishes might include *haricots verts* [green beans]; asparagus, white or green; or the traditional *pommes sarladaises* [potatoes cooked in duck fat].

LE FROMAGE

A variety of cheese is offered to guests after the main course is finished. It will be served on a separate plate, and there will be a choice of three or four types. *Cabécou de Rocamadour*, a small goat cheese round, is common in the Dordogne. A wedge of cheese is cut lengthwise, and round cheese is cut by making wedges, much like slicing up a pie.

LE DESSERT

Dessert is always served in a private home. A fruit tart or scoop of sorbet in the summer is a refreshing end to a long meal.

LE CAFÉ

Coffee comes after dessert, not with it, in France and is usually a small espresso. A *café normal* will get you a regular-size coffee and a cappuccino is the same in every language, though sometimes it is served with whipped cream instead of milk foam. Tea is also an option.

LE POUSSE-CAFÉ

Literally meaning "the coffee pusher," the *pousse-café* is a digestif, such as brandy, that is offered after coffee.

❧ DINING CUSTOMS AND TRADITIONS ❧

ONCE SEATED, it might be handy to know what's expected of you at the table. As a general rule, just be polite and respectful, as with any dining experience. Here are a few dining customs you might encounter in the Dordogne:

- Keep your hands above the table, without resting your elbows on the table. This is a hard one to get used to for those taught to fold their hands neatly on their laps. The thought behind this is, if your hands aren't above the table, where are they, and what are they doing?

- *Faire Chabrol.* This uniquely *Périgourdine* custom requires that you pour a small amount of red wine into the dregs of your soup bowl, then—bottoms up!

- Never spread foie gras. Always cut it and place in on your piece of bread to eat.

- The last drop from the wine bottle should be given to the single person at the table. It is believed that whoever has the last drop will be married that year.

- If invited to a French home for a meal, the general rule is to arrive fifteen minutes after the expected time. The further south you go in France, the more flexible the tardiness.

- Bringing a hostess gift is not expected. If you do, chocolates are a good choice. Wine is likely to have been chosen by your host; flowers are complicated.

- Should you decide to bring flowers, avoid chrysanthemums, which are brought to cemeteries; carnations, which express bad will; and red roses, which are reserved for lovers. A bouquet should contain an odd number of blooms, but not thirteen. All-white flowers are appropriate for weddings and funerals only.

- At one time, it was considered inappropriate for a woman to serve herself wine at the table if there is an able-bodied man who can do it for her. In today's world, this out-of-date custom is probably relegated to formal dinner parties at the palace.

- While it is common to say, "Bon appétit" to fellow Anglophones, it is generally not said at a French table, and never said at a posh dinner party.

- Dress appropriately. The French version of casual never involves flip-flops, jogging pants, or a New York Yankees baseball cap.

- In France, if using both the fork and the knife, the fork is held in the left hand and the knife in the right.

Whether you are dining in a private home or in a fine restaurant, one thing is a given: the meal is created and presented with care. Meals in France are drawn out for the purpose of enjoyment—civilized loitering, if you will. There is much to observe over the course of a meal, about the people around you, about the origins of the customs, and about the food itself. So sit back, relax, and enjoy the lessons of the table. Just keep your hands where we can see them.

COLLOQUIAL EXPRESSIONS
RELATED TO FOOD/EATING/COOKING

French Expression	English Equivalent
avoir du pain sur la planche =	to have your work cut out for you
raconter des salades =	to tell lies or tall tales
Ce n'est pas tes oignons =	It's none of your business.
un oeil au beurre noir =	a black eye
tomber dans les pommes =	to faint
mettre les pieds dans le plat =	to put one's foot in one's mouth
avoir les foies =	to have cold feet; to be scared stiff
être au four et au moulin =	to be in two places at once
faire bouillir la marmite =	to bring home the bacon
tondre des oeufs =	to be cheap; stingy
un pot de vin =	a bribe
avoir de la brioche =	to have a gut; a spare tire
C'est du gateau! =	It's a piece of cake!

Chapter 1

The Crown Jewels

W AS it really Peter Mayle's tome *A Year in Provence* that prompted that region's popularity surge over the last fifteen years? Would Monaco have been on the map for anyone other than yachtsmen and bankers if Grace Kelly hadn't transformed from Hollywood queen to real-life royal? While the Dordogne may not have a famous book (yet) or a celebrity princess to put its name in lights, it is home to many of France's epicurean stars and is recognized by chefs and gourmets the world over. So why is the Dordogne not smothered in tourists? Not that we should complain; the near-empty roads let us keep the black Périgord truffles, duck, and foie gras all to ourselves. While these luxuries are considered the jewels of France's culinary crown, in the Dordogne they are also linked to its tradition and history.

Aphrodisiacal and medicinal powers have been attributed to the truffle since Greek and Roman times. Over the centuries they have maintained their mystique while becoming an integral part of French cuisine. Today, the most valuable truffle groves, or *truffières,* are located in the Périgord and Provence regions of France. While several truffle varieties are found around the world, it is the *Tuber melanosporum* (black Périgord truffle) that gives the subterranean mushroom its superstar status and reputation. Known as "black diamonds" due to their high price and rarity, these beauties grow among the roots of many species

The Black Périgord Truffle (Black Gold) is coveted by chefs and connoisseurs around the world.

of tree, predominantly oak. The annual French harvest has tumbled steadily, and prices have skyrocketed in response. Production in 2004–05 was about ten tons, and the retail price in Paris reached $4,200 per kilo. Truffles mature between December 1 and March 31, and the famous market in Saint-Alvère is the place to buy them. Despite their lumpy, globular appearance, the black Périgord truffle is among the world's most coveted food items.

We met Hugues Martin near Saint-Alvère, where we followed him and his little dog around his thirty-acre grove, Truffière Bressac. We felt like characters in a John Le Carré novel as Hughes regaled us with stories of truffle poachers and an unexpected visit from Croatian truffle buyers dressed in dark suits. Hughes' passion for the trade is tireless and infectious. He hunts truffles with his dog but says some farmers use pigs, which can be risky, since pigs like to eat their finds. Still others search by the fly—yes, a truffle fly. This species of *mouche* (fly) smells a truffle when it is appropriately ripe, then lays its eggs on the site, as opposed to dogs, which can smell a truffle before it is mature. A perfect truffle, advises Hughes, should be firm, not too mushy, with a good aroma. Truffles harvested too early or too late can mean bad sales at the market. "The fly never lies," he quips.

Though our intrigue with truffles was heightened to new levels thanks to Hughes and his truffle tales, there is no denying that in the Dordogne duck is king. There are dozens of ways to prepare duck and its cousin the goose. After reading hundreds of menus and trying our own recipes, we found that not much is wasted when it comes to these feathered friends. *Magret*, the steaklike breast, is served roasted and sliced (delicious) or smoked in a salad. The neck is stuffed and baked to make *cou farci*; gizzards, or *gésiers*, are often found in salads. The carcass is used to make soup stock, and, as one farmer explained, "the feathers go to the beds and the bones to the dogs."

The legs of the duck are renowned in the Dordogne, and it is virtually impossible to visit a restaurant without seeing (and smelling) *confit de canard*, or duck confit, a duck leg fried to a crispy, golden brown, on the menu. From our very first bite more than ten years ago, we were hooked on this deceptively simple dish whose preparation is anything but. The French word *confit* means preserved, and before the advent of refrigeration, farmers preserved meat in fat and stored it in ceramic jars to get through long periods of time and food shortages. To make confit, the duck is cured in salt, garlic, and spices, and slowly poached in fat for up to nine hours. This is a time-consuming and dwindling culinary art. Fortunately, there are plenty of family chefs around the Dordogne who uphold the ancient tradition.

Hughes Martin

ALONG the Vézère River that meanders between Le Bugue and Montignac, history unfurls. A drive from point to point reveals stunning landscapes and massive limestone cliffs punctured with numerous grottoes and caves that were occupied by ancient man more than fifty-five thousand years ago (Cro-Magnon man is Dordogne's most famous resident after all). On September 12, 1940, near the village of Montignac, four teenagers discovered the world-famous Lascaux caves, where paintings date from between 15,000 and 13,000 BC. The original caves were closed permanently to the public in 1963, but in 1983 a replica called Lascaux II, with facsimiles of the paintings re-created down to the millimeter, was opened about two hundred meters from the original site. Local artist Monique Peytral was part of the team that spent eleven years completing the work.

We entered the caves for the first time not expecting to be impressed, but as we blinked and squinted to adjust to the darkness, shapeless images morphed into prehistoric pictures of horses and cows, and an ancient man who once stood where we did. Though it was a facsimile, no detail was spared in re-creating these images, all done with a meticu-lous and scientific approach. We were mesmerized, feeling as if we had discovered them ourselves. The Museum of Pre-history (*Musée Nationale de Préhistoire*) in Les Eyzies-de-Tayac-Sireuil offers a comprehensive display of artifacts and fossils, as well as a caveman's view above the valley. Halfway between Les Eyzies and Montignac, the limestone rock of Saint Christophe (*La Roque Saint-Christophe*) juts out of the landscape and is an imposing one kilometer (over a half mile) long and eighty meters (262 feet) high, with wide views over the river valley. The area is also home to numerous underground caverns, like Proumeyssac in Le Bugue, the largest in the Dordogne and referred to as the Crystal Cathedral because of its amazing stalagmites and crystalline formations. Here a basket lowers you into the dark cavern to experience its discovery the way the first explorers did. (Or you can walk down, like the rest of us.)

Wherever you end up in the Vézère Valley, you will be walking in the footsteps of some very old Dordogne residents (Cro-Magnon man and Neanderthal man were here). Tens of thousands of years of history are still on display. One thing is certain—wherever you explore along this green valley, you're sure to feel young! ∎

We don't want to ruffle any feathers (pun intended; hold the wise quacks), but to overlook foie gras when talking about Périgord cuisine would be like not mentioning gumbo when discussing the cooking in New Orleans. *Foie gras,* which means "fat liver," is one of the most savored elements in French cuisine, and the production of the buttery delicacy is as much a part of Dordogne history as the brooding castles and bastides. The *gavage,* the controversial technique of force-feeding geese or duck to fatten their livers, dates back to ancient Egyptians and Romans, but it was as a French specialty that it transfixed the discerning palates of the world. The delicacy has its French origins in Strasbourg, though it has been produced on small Dordogne farms for generations. Major commercial production of foie gras moved to the region after World War II. Today, France produces roughly 80 percent of the world's foie gras, the majority of which hails from the Dordogne. It's still possible to visit small farms where geese and duck are raised for the production of foie gras. In many of the old photographs

and postcards of ancient Périgord, it is the women you will see tending to and feeding the fowl. Unlike many businesses and farm activities, the *gavage* was primarily the woman's job and a skill passed down from mothers to daughters. Farms like *La Ferme de Biorne* near Bergerac and *La Borderie* in Chavagnac, run by our friend Danièle, offer cooking classes for those who want to understand the process and learn to prepare the world-famous delicacy.

Foie gras can be bought *cru* (raw) or prepared into a terrine or pâté that is excellent served cold with toast and fruit compote. Many restaurants also serve it *poêlé* (pan seared) with figs or prunes, or on crisp, green asparagus, like at the restaurant L'Essentiel in Perigueux. But the real question is: duck or goose? Connoisseurs allege goose foie gras to be superior, claiming a more delicate flavor. However, there are

Jean-Pierre Bordier in his waterfall-powered mill.

those who prefer the more rustic taste of duck foie gras, so it really comes down to personal preference. Roughly 95 percent of the foie gras produced in France comes from ducks. Whether or not you decide to eat it is up to you, but foie gras can't be ignored as an essential part of French gastronomy and Périgord history.

With our stomachs as a constant guide, we discovered another gustatory jewel worthy of a place in the Dordogne's culinary crown: the walnut (*noix*). It may not be considered as top flight as the region's truffles or foie gras, but this little brown nut packs a mighty flavor, and evidence of its existence in the region goes back more than ten thousand years. During the fall, the trees are encumbered with nuts, and restaurants and markets swell with walnut products, including oil, mustard, wine, and, our favorite, walnut cake. We visited the Moulin de la Tour in Sainte-Nathalène, where owner Jean-Pierre Bordier has worked for twenty-eight years. Before him, his father-in-law ran the sixteenth-century mill. Even though we showed up on a day when they were closed, we tracked the jolly Jean-Pierre down in his orchard, and he gladly welcomed us in and showed us around the only water-powered mill in the Dordogne. In 2002 four Périgord nut varieties were granted official *Appelation d'origine contrôlée* (AOC) status—a sign that things will only get nuttier in the Dordogne.

It is widely acknowledged that France is the apex of haute cuisine today (don't tell the Italians), but who really understands the true genesis of the phenomenon? Personally, we think its origins are here in the Dordogne. It's a region best visited by mouth, where France's culinary kings and epicurean jewels have reigned for thousands of years—and still do.

Walnuts are crushed under a grinding stone to create
a paste at Moulin de la Tour.

⋙ THE INDELIBLE DÁNIÈLE ⋘

"Cooking is so much more than just eating."

WHEN WE FIRST approached the seven-hundred-year-old farmhouse of Danièle Mazet-Delpeuch, we weren't sure we had come to the right place. The address she had given us was simply La Borderie, in a blink of a village called Chavagnac. Only a small wooden sign reassured us we were on the right path. As we made our way down a pitted road, past overgrown oaks and fig trees brimming with fruit, and up to a stone cottage dressed in lace curtains, we wondered if we had fallen into Périgord of yesteryear. Once inside, we knew we had.

The house where Danièle's father was born, where her four children were raised, and where she welcomes her six grandchildren each summer, could be a movie set. Straw hats hang from one of the wooden beams, and an old-fashioned lamp provides light to a small workspace where Danièle has laid out a crisply ironed white cloth on which she slices smoked *sanglier* (wild boar) with a small paring knife that she points at us when she talks. "I live almost like my grandmother did," she says.

The house is indeed untouched by time, and she confirms that not much has changed, except for refrigeration and plumbing. The main room is tidy and consists of the kitchen, dining, and living areas, and a sliding door that leads to an overgrown garden. But the pièce de résistance and our biggest source of curiosity is the enormous fireplace dominating the room. It is open on both sides, with a slew of cooking utensils at the ready. Danièle stokes the flames and tells us she designed the fireplace herself with a purpose. "Cooking is so much more than just eating," she says. "It is talking and being social, and making people as happy as you can with the food you prepare."

Danièle picks up a black cast-iron pot called a *royale* and sets it down in the embers. She tells us it is more than one hundred years old. "The trick is, you never wash them," she says, wiping the pot with a cloth. When we ask her what she cooks in it, she says, "Everything—a whole turkey, a *lièvre* (wild hare), a cake." With that, she takes a paintbrush, dips it in goose fat and coats the inside of the *royale*. Within minutes the familiar aroma permeates the house. The fireplace is almost large enough to stand in, and we wonder if she ever hangs geese or lamb from the ominous hooks dangling from the dark void in the chimney. "No, that's cooking for tourists," she says with a laugh.

Danièle has a no-nonsense air about her, and she slips between English and French every few sentences. She also talks with her hands—and whatever is in them (sharp knife, fork, hot fireplace poker). Her grace and elegance were apparent from the moment we met, so it's no surprise her table is regularly surrounded by friends, family, or journalists curious about this local legend. Today she has invited a radio show host from Santa Rosa, California, and his wife, along with friends who own a bed-and-breakfast nearby. She is busily preparing lunch but makes time to serve us coffee, then hurries to the garden to pluck some figs from her tree for the *amuse-bouche*. Danièle invites us to stay for the midday meal, but we decline, feeling bad that we have come at such a hectic time.

"You know," she says, pointing at us with the knife she is now using to slice figs, "If you make an appointment for eleven in the morning here in the Périgord, it is expected you will have something to eat." She tells us this courteous custom stems from times when people would travel four to five days by horse and carriage. Even though we have come only two hours by car, we gladly change our minds and accept her invitation. With a pleased nod, Danièle takes a dish of potatoes from her counter and excuses herself to warm them in the oven located in the demonstration kitchen next door.

As we look around more closely, mostly to verify that there really is no oven in the room, Danièle is revealed to us in snippets. The walls are covered in signed oil paintings and mementos. Above the heavy wooden door hang old wicker baskets used for gathering fruit from her trees and shopping at the markets, while several unusual-looking cooking utensils lie strewn around the smoldering fireplace ashes. On a rickety antique table, two photo albums bulge with magazine articles and photos that span Danièle's past twenty years. Dozens of jars of homemade confiture sit half-full on the wooden buffet below white lace curtains, and homemade cakes and pies under glass domes look as if they have been recently sliced. We concede that her life is simple, but it is certainly not empty.

In 1975 Danièle began Foie Gras Weekends, a three-day course teaching visitors about the region's cuisine. Even today she offers cooking classes and gourmet tours from her family home. In 1979 she founded the École d'Art et Tradition Culinaire du Périgord, the region's first cooking school. These endeavors earned her a formidable reputation and several awards, including the *Chevalier du Mérite Agricole* from the French agricultural industry, an award rarely bestowed upon a woman. But, then again, this is no ordinary woman. Danièle is most commonly asked (including by us) about her two years (1988–1990) as personal chef for François Mitterrand, the late president of France. "I suppose I will always be remembered as that, more than anything else I have done," she acknowledges.

But her gastronomic life goes beyond the presidential palace in Paris and has taken her around the world as a lecturer, teacher, and chef, to places as diverse as China, Mexico, New York, Montreal, Moscow, and Sydney. She's even worked in Antarctica, where she spent fourteen months cooking at a research lab and celebrated the millennium and her sixtieth birthday. "I was looking for a change," she says. "But, it's always nice to come back to roots."

Danièle is setting out jewel-toned apéritif glasses. Her table is covered with a well-used tablecloth and is set with dishes embellished with an autumn motif. From a heavy wooden chest of drawers, she pulls out water and wine glasses and arranges them in their proper positions; from another drawer she removes the cutlery and sets it piece by piece on the table, the forks laid tines down. "This is the French way," she says. "The tines go down so that guests can see the family crest on the back of the silverware." We ask if she always goes to such lengths when setting the table. "But, of course. It is the least I can do to welcome my guests."

Danièle slowly circles the table and looks up to comment on the brightly colored paintings we are admiring, pointing a fork in our direction. "Those are painted by

Monique Peytral, who painted the facsimiles of the Lascaux caves," she said. "She is a very good friend of mine and was just here for dinner."

Back over at the fire, the duck legs are beginning to sizzle in the *royale*, and Danièle transfers them to a platter. She leaves to retrieve the warmed potatoes, which would be the most heavenly we have ever tasted, made with cream, *cèpes* (porcini mushrooms), and cheese, and cooked the night before underneath a roasted lamb. Like an elegant *pas de deux*, platters of pâté and figs stuffed with *sanglier* arrive on the table just as Danièle's guests arrive. We toast and sip our *vin de noix* (walnut wine), and ask Danièle what's next for her. As expected, she has some ideas swirling about her. Her latest passion is truffles and a project to bring truffles to New Zealand, but she clarifies, pointing her index finger at the sky, "The real *truffe*, the *Tuber melanosporum* from Périgord."

Danièle said earlier that she is likely to be remembered as the ex-cook for the ex-president of France, but one need only spend an afternoon with her to discover she is so much more. She is a mother, a grandmother, a teacher, an explorer, a friend, a truffle lobbyist, a gracious hostess, and a passionate ambassador of all things Périgord. It was an honor to have her fork pointed at us. ■

Danièle's Nems
with Duck Foie Gras

"In my *Périgourdine* kitchen, flavors are often borrowed from the various countries I visit or from the travelers that I meet. These *nems* (Parisian term for Vietnamese rolls) with duck foie gras are inspired by my friend Gabrielle from Lyon, who was born in Vietnam in 1920." ~Danièle

MAKES 10 ROLLS

1 tablespoon (14 g) goose fat

1 white onion, thinly sliced

2 small zucchini, finely julienned

1 garlic clove, minced

1 tablespoon (15 ml) soy sauce

¼ pound (100 g) raw foie gras

1 tablespoon (15 ml) red wine vinegar

10 rice paper circles (spring roll wrappers) for nem wrappers

4 cups (1 liter) vegetable oil

In a frying pan, melt the duck fat over medium-high heat. Add the onion and sauté until soft and translucent, about 10 minutes. Add the zucchini and garlic and cook another 5 minutes. Add the soy sauce, reduce the heat to low, and simmer for 2 minutes. Set aside.

To prepare the nems, cut the foie gras into pieces approximately 2 inches long and sprinkle them with the red wine vinegar.

Fill a bowl with cool water. Dip each rice paper circle into the water, then set on a clean surface. Place about 1 tablespoon of the onion-zucchini mixture and 1 piece of the foie gras in the center of the dampened rice paper. Roll the rice paper over the filling while tucking in the sides to make a "cigar-shaped" cylinder. Place seam-side down on plastic wrap and repeat until all of the rolls have been made. It is best to fry the rolls right away.

Heat the oil in a fryer or medium saucepan until it reaches 350°F (180°C) on a deep-fry thermometer. Fry the nems in the hot oil until golden brown, about 3 to 4 minutes.

Serve with a sweet and sour dipping sauce and a crisp seasonal salad.

Sauce Périgueux

This rich sauce flavored with Madeira wine and truffles is known as the king of sauces and is the pinnacle of gastronomic pedigree and haute cuisine. Named after the Dordogne city of Périgueux, the sauce is delicious served over a tender grilled filet of beef with a great glass of wine—and in good company.

———————————◆◖◆◗◆———————————

MAKES 6 SERVINGS

1 tablespoon (14 g) goose fat
or shortening

1 large shallot, chopped

½ cup (125 ml) Madeira

½ cup (125 ml) cognac or brandy

4 cups (1 liter) beef or veal stock

3 tablespoons (43 g) unsalted butter,
softened, divided

2 tablespoons (12.5 g) all-purpose flour

1 medium black truffle
(about 60 g), minced

Coarse salt and cracked pepper

In a medium saucepan over medium heat, melt the goose fat. Add the shallot and cook until lightly browned, 10 to 12 minutes. Add the Madeira and cognac and simmer until the liquors reduce by half, 2 to 3 minutes. Add the stock and simmer for 15 to 20 minutes longer.

In a small bowl, mix together 2 tablespoons of the butter and the flour to make a paste.

Strain the sauce through a sieve, then return the sauce to the heat and bring to a simmer. Whisk in some of the flour paste, stirring constantly, until the sauce slightly thickens. Add more of the flour paste, as needed, to thicken the sauce. Stir in the minced truffle and the remaining 1 tablespoon butter and season with salt and pepper.

Serve the sauce spooned over meat or on the side.

Salade Périgourdine

This is a regional classic prepared with giblets, walnuts, and thin slices of smoked duck breast. We love the addition of warm croutons with goat cheese. Dressed with nutty walnut vinaigrette and garnished with tomatoes, this version is our favorite of all the salads we've enjoyed in the Dordogne.

––––––––––––––––– ❦ –––––––––––––––––

To make the vinaigrette, in a small bowl, whisk the oil into the vinegar. Season with salt and pepper. Set aside.

To make the salad, preheat the oven to 375°F (190°C).

Drain the giblets. In a small frying pan over medium-high heat, cook the giblets until brown, about 15 minutes. Keep warm.

Lightly spread the butter on the baguette slices. Place the baguette slices, buttered side up, on a baking sheet and bake until very lightly toasted, 3 to 4 minutes. Remove the baking sheet from the oven and top each baguette slice with 1 piece of goat cheese. Return to the oven and bake until the cheese begins to melt, about 5 minutes.

Divide the greens evenly among 4 large plates. Top each salad with a few slices of smoked duck breast, some warm giblets, a few tomato wedges, 2 goat cheese croutons, and a few prunes (if desired). Scatter with the toasted walnuts and drizzle with the walnut vinaigrette.

MAKES 4 SERVINGS

For the vinaigrette:

½ cup (125 ml) good-quality walnut oil

3 tablespoons (45 ml) walnut vinegar

Coarse salt and cracked pepper

For the salad:

1 can (5 oz/155 g) preserved giblets

1 tablespoon (14 g) unsalted butter, softened

8 baguette slices, each about 1½ inches (4 cm) thick

¼ pound (125 g) fresh goat cheese, preferably cabécou, cut into 8 pieces

8 cups (225 g) mixed salad greens

½ pound (250 g) smoked duck breast, thinly sliced

4 medium tomatoes, cut into wedges

24 dried prunes (optional)

1 cup (125 g) shelled walnuts, toasted

Confit de Canard

Danièle Mazet-Delpeuch prepares this dish employing traditional methods her grandmother used, making it even more enjoyable for us. By starting with whole ducks, you can render the necessary fat and supplement with shortening, or order goose fat from numerous online sites (see Resource Guide). You can use the leftover bones to make a rich duck stock and save the breast for another meal.

To remove the breast from the duck, use a heavy boning knife to carefully cut the breast meat from each side of the duck, starting at the top of the breastbone. Loosen the meat from the bones and cut down to the thigh. Insert the knife into the thigh joint to remove the leg and thigh in one piece. Reserve any pieces of excess fat.

Place the legs and thighs in an airtight container; reserve the duck carcasses and breasts for another recipe. Add the salt, pepper, thyme, and garlic and rub well into the meat. Cover and refrigerate for 24 to 48 hours.

In a small saucepan over low heat, melt the reserved duck fat trimmings. Pour the rendered fat into a container, cover, and refrigerate.

After the duck has marinated, rinse each piece under cold water and pat dry with paper towels. Place the duck in a large Dutch oven and cover with the rendered duck fat, adding additional fat as needed to make 4 to 6 cups (1 to 1.5 kg) total. Cover and cook over low heat until fork tender, about 2 hours. Let cool to room temperature. Transfer the duck meat and fat to an airtight container, making sure that the fat completely covers the meat. Cover and refrigerate 3 to 4 days to preserve.

At this point the duck confit can be stored for up to 2 weeks in the refrigerator for use in other recipes or prepared as follows:

Remove the duck pieces and scrape off most of the fat. In a large, heavy frying pan over medium heat, working in batches, cook the legs until the skin is crispy and brown, about 10 minutes per side. Pour off most of the fat as you are cooking.

Serve right away with *Pommes Sarladaise* (page 48).

MAKES 8 SERVINGS

4 whole ducklings
(4 to 5 lb/2 to 2.5 kg each)

½ cup (120 g) coarse salt

3 tablespoons cracked pepper

2 teaspoons dried
(or 4 sprigs fresh) thyme

5 garlic cloves, minced

4 to 6 cups (1 to 1.5 kg) goose fat
or shortening

Pommes Sarladaise

The mouthwatering smell of potatoes cooking in goose fat wafts through the village of Sarlat, famous for its weekly market, slate rooftops, and foie gras. The duet of *duck confit* and these heavenly spuds ranks high among the region's best comfort food.

———— ❦ ————

In a large, heavy frying pan over medium heat, melt the fat. Add the potatoes and season with salt and pepper. Cook, turning the potatoes to coat well, for 5 minutes.

Reduce the heat and continue cooking until the potatoes are browned and soft, 20 to 30 minutes. Stir in the garlic and parsley and cook for 5 minutes longer. Serve right away.

MAKES 6 SERVINGS

4 tablespoons (60 g) goose fat
or shortening

1½ pounds (750 g) russet potatoes,
peeled and sliced ¾ inch (2 cm) thick

Coarse salt and cracked pepper

3 garlic cloves, minced

3 tablespoons chopped fresh parsley

Walnut Crème Brûlée

Sweet dark walnut liquor is floated on the finished crème brûlée for an unexpected taste that's pure Dordogne decadence.

———————————————◆◆———————————————

Preheat the oven to 275°F (135°C). Have ready four ramekins and a large roasting pan.

In a medium bowl, beat the granulated sugar, egg yolks, and vanilla until light.

In a saucepan over medium heat, warm the cream until small bubbles appear along the edge of the pan. Slowly pour a small amount of the cream into the egg yolk mixture, stirring constantly. Stir the remaining cream into the mixture and mix well.

Pour the custard into the ramekins. Set the ramekins inside the roasting pan and pour hot water into the pan to reach halfway up the sides of the ramekins. Bake until a small thin knife inserted in the center of the custard comes out clean, about 45 minutes.

Carefully remove the pan from the oven. When the ramekins are cool enough to handle, lift them out of the water bath and let cool for about 15 minutes. Cover with plastic wrap placed directly over the surface of the custard to prevent a skin from forming. Refrigerate until chilled, about 1 hour or overnight.

In a small bowl, mix together the light and dark brown sugars. Sprinkle a thin layer of the sugar mixture on top of each custard. Using a small kitchen torch, caramelize the sugar until set. Pour 1 tablespoon of the walnut liquor over each custard and serve.

Note: If you don't have a kitchen torch, you can caramelize the sugar by broiling the brulée on the top rack. Watch them to make sure the sugar doesn't burn.

MAKES 4 SERVINGS

½ cup (125 g) granulated sugar

5 extra-large egg yolks

1 tablespoon (15 ml) vanilla extract

2 cups (500 ml) heavy whipping cream

¼ cup (60 g) firmly packed light
brown sugar

¼ cup (60 g) firmly packed dark
brown sugar

¼ cup (60 ml) walnut liquor,
preferably La Vieille Noix
(see headnote on page 94)

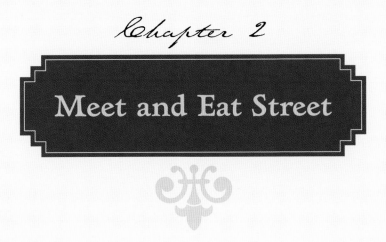

Chapter 2

Meet and Eat Street

ONE of the greatest pleasures of travel in France is discovering the local dishes, and a tour of any local farmhouse inn or market is proof that regional cooking is alive and well. Food and socializing are culturally important in France, so it makes sense the two go hand in hand, especially here in the Dordogne, a region enjoyed as much for its gustatory pleasures as its warmhearted welcomes. And nowhere is this marriage of food and friendship more evident than at the colorful outdoor markets that are in full swing every day, and where the activity du jour is meeting and eating.

The Sunday market in Issigeac fills the narrow medieval streets around a sixteenth-century church and the seventeenth-century bishop's palace and is among our "must dos" each time we come. If it's not the scent of the rotisserie chicken or the aroma of the fresh plucked strawberries that draw us to the main square, it's the exceptional variety of local wines, meat, fruit, and vegetables that make it worth any food lover's trouble, even if it's just to sniff and stare. Issigeac is truly a "locals" market, with a reputation for being among the best in the region, and is frequented by locals and perennial visitors like us. Coming here is like coming home for us; familiar faces smile and eyebrows raise in genuine delight at seeing us again. Not much changes here, even the location of the vendors, and this familiarity is the charm of shopping the outdoor markets. We know we'll always find the chicken guys next to the church, Dominique and her *canelés* too, and our

Market day in the medieval village of Sarlat is a pilgrimage for visitors and locals.

favorite cheesemonger is forever slicing up his walnut-infused variety just outside the art gallery on the main square. The bastide of Villereal holds a market on Saturday and it is a must stop even in the off-season. We get the sense that, unlike Issigeac, Villereal is really "lived in" rather than just frequented by outliers. There seems to be a weekly event under the medieval market *halle*, be it a nocturnal market, a wine festival, or a community bodega (village street party). On market day, socializing takes center stage, with dozens of cafés lining the market square and the streets, full of chattering locals, sipping coffee and sometimes even an aperitif (yes, even at 10 a.m.). Our kind of people. Many markets, like Sarlat, are part of the tourist pilgrimage through the region, especially during the summer months. We certainly won't discourage you from visiting Sarlat. It is, after all, one of the most visited towns in the region for good reason, but on market day, we recommend you also visit the smaller villages, whose markets

fly below the tour bus radar yet don't skimp on delicious surprises. On a Tuesday in Le Bugue, we discovered unusual home-cured sausages we had never seen before elsewhere. About the size of a small goat cheese round, the delicious sausage is cut with an *Opinel* (a pocketknife every Frenchman seems to have at the ready in case a picnic breaks out) and handed out to lucky passersby. Thursday in Lalinde revealed the unusual *tourteau fromagé*, a French cheesecake with a distinct charcoal-black crust, something we had never seen in all our visits to the region. Like many of the markets, Lalinde serves up spontaneous entertainment. Here, a guitarist, a poetry reading, or an impromptu concert is not an uncommon soundtrack to the lively market scenes that flicker by. One of the most popular and most visited markets in the Dordogne is Sarlat. Each year, more than a million visitors descend on this town of ten thousand. The maze of alleyways, beautifully preserved since the Middle Ages, and the stone houses capped with gray slate roofs, are among the main draws, but it's the Saturday market that lures us back year after year.

DURING the summer, a handful of the market towns also host *marchés nocturnes* (night markets). These outings are a fun and novel way to experience local fare and culture. Not every town holds a night market, but signs advertising *marchés nocturnes* are usually posted on the roads or in the villages proper. Better yet, check with the shop owners or ask the vendors during the morning market. They are often the keepers of great advice.

During the evening markets, tables are set up around the central square, and vendors sell everything you need for a good meal, including the wine, which they will happily uncork and pour into plastic cups. There is usually live music or a DJ, and dancing, to encourage visitors to savor the flavors of the region well into the evening, which is what we did one summer night in Villefranche-du-Périgord.

While cutting into some goat cheese one evening, we were jolted from our wine-induced calm by an eruption of song from a nearby table. These hymns were clearly part of Dordogne patrimony, sung in a deep proud voice that made us want to put our hands over our hearts. This group of eight or so friends swayed and crooned in their best voices, and we felt severely unpatriotic. One by one, other tables stood and joined in. It wasn't long before we were the only table not standing. Though we couldn't keep up (we imagined "99 bottles of beer on the wall" wouldn't suffice), it didn't take away from the feeling that we were sharing something personal with these nameless revelers. Before we knew it, two ladies grabbed us, and soon we were linked arm in arm with our new friends, laughing, miming words, and pretending for the night that we were one of them. The rest of the evening was spent dancing under the halle with people we were sure we'd never see again, yet whom we would remember forever. ∎

TOWN	DAYS	TOWN	DAYS
Audrix	*Saturday*	Rouffignac	*Sunday, Wednesday*
Auriac-du-Périgord	*Thursday*	Salignac-Eyvigues	*Tuesday, Friday*
Bouzic	*Tuesday*	St. Amand de Coly	*Tuesday*
Bourdeilles	*Wednesday*	Valojoulx	*Friday*
Loubejac	*Thursday*	Varaignes	*Tuesday*
Peyrignac	*Friday*	Villefranche-du-Périgord	*Saturday, Tuesday*

On a quest to find the perfect truffle one summer, Laura and I split up for the scavenger hunt. Like an expert, she sniffed out the alluring mushroom. Before I could even say "*Avez-vous des truffes?*" she was giddily skipping toward me, shaking a white bag up and down. "It's just a summer truffle but it will do," she said with a smile, clearly satisfied with her find. We were equally satisfied at the table when Laura's Sarlat treasure was shaved over a bowl of pasta and served as our *entrée*. The foie gras produced in the area is among the most highly rated in France and has contributed to the culinary clout of the Dordogne. The market draws merchants selling local specialties, such as walnuts, duck, and truffles, as well as international products, like African spices, Italian olives, and Spanish paella. Delicious smells hang in the air here. If Sarlat were a cartoon, we'd be the characters hooked by the nose and lured from place to place by the swirling aroma cloud. We discovered there is no shortage of vendors and shops whose owners extend a toothpick or two with some delicious nibble speared onto the end.

While each market offers its own unique products and specialties, one thing you can consistently count on across them all is high-quality, fresh food direct from the grower. On display at a typical Dordogne market is a kaleidoscope of colorful fruits and vegetables, seafood pulled fresh from local rivers and the sea, *cabécou de Rocamadour* (a creamy goat cheese certified with the prestigious AOC, homemade liqueurs, and cakes). These are only a fragment of the goodies for sale. As the seasons change, so does the inventory. Delicious rotations of honey in summer, walnuts in fall, and the prized black Périgord truffle in winter make the region a year-round paradise for gourmets. Monpazier and Villefranche-du-Périgord are home to the world-famous *cèpes* (porcini mushrooms) markets early each fall, usually in September, but the exact timing depends on the weather. The *cèpes* markets take place all day every day as long as the *cèpes* last; then they disappear, as fast as they appear. We stopped by Monpazier on a crisp Thursday afternoon one autumn hoping to see overflowing bins of

supersized mushrooms but encountered an empty market square. We asked an erudite man in a flat, black hat if the market would come soon. He instructed us to come back "when the moon is just right after a nice rain." He shuffled off, laughing, leaving us to wonder if he was serious or just pulling our leg.

If you want a chance to meet the vendors and taste and touch the products, arriving before 7:30 a.m. to any market is a must. Trust us: it's worth setting the alarm. Early arrival not only gives you a shot at finding a parking space, but also guarantees a peek at an essential part of life in the Dordogne. Upon closer examination (and countless hours at nearby cafés), it is obvious to us the markets are about more than just commerce. The vagabond gourmets manning the market stalls are often from the third or fourth generation of families selling their goods, and friends and neighbors from local and far-off villages come to share news and catch up on the latest gossip. At the Sunday market in Saint-Cyprien, we saw a proud papa sharing photos of a new baby, while a nearby fruit vendor yelled his bonjours to fellow hawkers, and a pair of well-dressed ladies hooked arms and twittered incessantly, like long-lost sisters.

Each time we come to the Dordogne, we do as the locals do and frequent the same markets and find familiar faces in the exact spot we left them the time before. We share our own news and updates, and busy or not, we join a few people for coffee at a nearby café, just because that's what you do. Market day in the Dordogne is special, and the connection is something you can't get from a onetime visit.

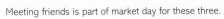
Meeting friends is part of market day for these three.

MARKET MENU

A daily slice of markets around the Dordogne.

MONDAY

Les Eyzies de Tayac, Sainte Alvère, Le Fleix

TUESDAY

Brantôme, Le Bugue, Ribérac, Salignac, Thenon, Trémolat,
Beaumont-du-Perigord, Bergerac, Lisle

WEDNESDAY

Le Buisson-de-Cadouin, Gardonne, Hautefort, Montignac, Sarlat, Vélines,
La Tour Blanche, Périgueux, Bergerac

THURSDAY

Domme, Eymet, Lalinde, Monpazier, Terrasson-Lavilledieu, La Force,
Meyrals, La Coquille, Saint-Astier

FRIDAY

Cubjac, Le Lardin-Saint-Lazare, Ribérac, Vergt, Sigoulès,
Brantôme, Le Buisson-de-Cadouin

SATURDAY

Belvès, Douzillac, Villereal, Sarlat, Thiviers, Villefranche-du-Périgord,
Saint-Pierre-de-Chignac, La Roche-Chalais, Saint-Léon sur l'Isle, Coulounieix-Chamiers

SUNDAY

Issigeac, Augignac, Couze-et-Saint-Front, Eymet, Saint-Cyprien, Singleyrac,
Sorges, Tourtoirac, Creysse, Daglan, La Douze, Gardonne

❧ THE CHICKEN GUYS ❧

THE CHICKEN GUYS and their rotisserie chickens are a staple at the markets in the Dordogne. In fact, they are so much a part of the market landscape that finding anyone to recall their actual names proves to be a real challenge. Their names, in fact, are Gilles and Gerard, but ask anyone, and they are the Chicken Guys. They drive more than three thousand miles each month to sixteen different markets a week. If you've spent any time in the Dordogne markets, you've probably seen them at least once.

It's an unusually cold and rainy morning when we track them down in Issigeac just outside the church. We had only to follow the smell of comfort food (aka anything fattening) to find them. In a rolling rotisserie truck, Gilles and Gerard roast rows upon rows of chicken, *poussin* (spring chicken), and quail. The birds turn and drip over garlic, onions, and potatoes until everything is crisp and golden brown. Chef Laura sees the chickens, and as if there is a cartoon bubble above her head, it is because she has drifted off into a vision of roasted chicken with truffles and a splash of sweet Monbazillac wine. We rub our cold hands together in front of the truck, accepting pieces of a roasted bird Gilles graciously carves for us. We comment to the pair how lucky they are to be working in front of a fire. "It's okay today," remarks Gilles, loading more raw chickens onto a spit, "But when it's summer and thirty degrees [Celsius; equals 86°F], it's not so great." He has a point, but it is hard to imagine hot weather while relentless rain is soaking our shoes.

Gilles and Gerard have been in the chicken business for twenty years, buying from local farms and heading out each morning before sunrise to get to their destinations, sometimes up to three different markets per day. We asked if he ever gets tired of that routine. Gilles gives the typical shoulder shrug and says, "That's the job." Each chicken sells for about 7 euros each, and Gilles and Gerard sell anywhere from 30 to 150 or more in a day, depending on the market and the weather. For anyone who makes a living like this, the correlation between a good business day and the weather is obvious: the better the weather, the more people at the markets to buy their products, especially on Saturday and Sunday.

There is not much foot traffic today, and we can see the vendors getting nervous and chatting among themselves. We stop to say hello to the always impeccably dressed Nicole, who sells succulent raspberries from her lone table-cloth-adorned table. Visibly distraught, though amazingly well clad, she waves her hands at the torrential rain and says, "This is killing us."

We asked Gilles how he thinks it's going to turn out today, and he gives us the typically French puff of the lips while raising his shoulders and turning his palms to the gray sky, "I don't know; I think it will be better tomorrow." We are reminded of Scarlett O'Hara's optimistic last words, "After all, tomorrow is another day." How appropriate this Southern belle's mantra is in the markets of Southern France. ▪

✤ HAMMING IT UP ✤

IN SEARCH OF a ham whose reputation made its way all the way to our dining table in Biron, we find Benoit Leseur in a preppy polo shirt at the Villereal market. Looking like an outsider, Benoit confirms that he left his desk job in Paris five years ago and headed south to the Dordogne. While he once carved up financial statements from nine to five, he now carves up ham for his business, Jambon à l'Os. It's quite a change, but that's just what he was after. "I came to the Dordogne for a different life," he explains. "A slower pace."

Different it is, but slower? We're not so sure. Benoit ventures out to Villereal and another four markets every week. While he is fortunate to live close to Villereal, other vendors travel up to one hundred miles to partake in the market. Benoit shops for his meats at local farms and prepares them all himself. At the markets, he sets up a delicious display of bubbling sauces, rotisserie pork, and ham carved right from the bone, handing out samples and calling out to unsuspecting shoppers. He smiles when he sees us and beckons us back for more tasting.

"I like meeting the people—the clients and the other vendors," he says. Though he admits competition is fierce, Benoit believes building relationships is all part of the requisite practice and fun of market life.

We have to believe Benoit has no competition to speak of. It's not often we get so excited about ham that we stalk it and its producer from market to market. But when it's this good, we just can't help ourselves. ∎

"I came to the Dordogne for a different life."

➽ THE SAVOR OF SUMMER ➼

NOTHING SAYS SUMMER like red, ripe strawberries. In pies and parfaits, on top of cakes, or alone in a bowl, the succulent red fruit brings back memories of younger days, when summer vacation was really a vacation. What a treat then it was to meet Nadine Gipoulou, whose hand-drawn sign reading "*mara des bois*" attracted our attention. It was love at first bite. This variety of strawberry has the intense flavor of the beloved *fraise des bois* (wild strawberry), but is larger, sweet, and juicy. We think it might just be the perfect strawberry, but we eat a half dozen more just to be sure. The *mara des bois* is a French creation that is beloved by growers because the plant produces so many berries. If you are lucky enough to be in France in August, you will see them at the markets, and Nadine always has a line in front of her overflowing table. She grows them organically on her farm near Monpazier, where she also makes confiture. The job is a hard one, she tells us, with each plant tended by hand. Nadine fears strawberry farming will soon disappear from France in favor of mass-produced berries from abroad. For her, strawberries are a family affair: she says her parents were the first to bring the *mara des bois* to the Dordogne. In hopes of carrying on the tradition, Nadine began bringing her own strawberries to market in 2000. Before that, she was a nurse. She jokes that now, instead of patients, she cares for strawberries because "they don't complain as much." No complaints from us either. With more *mara des bois* than we could possibly eat, we pop them into our mouths like candy, and revel in the memories of summers past. ◾

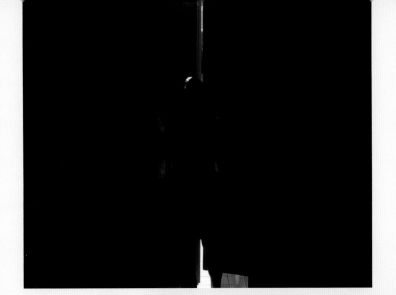

Warm Cabécou with Armagnac and Honey-Roasted Apricots

A marriage made in heaven using two of our favorite market delicacies: fresh apricots and *cabécou de Rocamadour*, a goat cheese with coveted AOC status. AOC or *appellation d'origine contrôlée* (controlled term of origin) is the certification given to French agricultural products, guaranteeing their authenticity. If you can't find *cabécou de Rocamadour*, any small goat cheese round will do.

Preheat the oven to 375°F (190°C).

Place the apricots, cut side down, on a baking sheet and drizzle with the Armagnac and honey. Bake until the apricots begin to soften but still hold their shape, 12 to 15 minutes.

Meanwhile, lightly spread the butter on the baguette slices. Place the baguette slices, buttered side up, on a baking sheet and bake until lightly toasted, about 10 minutes. Remove from the oven and top each slice with 1 cheese round. Return to the oven until the cheese begins to melt, about 5 minutes.

To serve, place each warm baguette slice on a salad plate and garnish with 4 roasted apricot halves.

MAKES 4 SERVINGS

8 fresh apricots, halved and pitted

¼ cup (60 ml) Armagnac

2 tablespoons (30 ml) good-quality honey

1 teaspoon (5 g) unsalted butter, softened

4 baguette slices, each about 1 inch (2.5 cm) thick

4 rounds *cabécou de Rocamadour* or other goat cheese

Sabine's Omelette with Cèpes

Market-fresh eggs achieve gastronomic grandeur in the Dordogne. Perhaps it's the hot goose fat in which the *cèpes* (porcini mushrooms) are sautéed or the addition of the *persillade*, an herb-garlic mixture that is always at the ready in Dordogne kitchens. If you can't find goose fat, you can substitute bacon drippings or unsalted butter. Our friend Sabine whom we met at the Restaurant du Chateau in Biron whipped up this simple omelette for us in minutes, but we savored the taste all day. She happily shared her recipe with us.

——————◆◆——————

To make the *persillade*, combine the garlic and parsley in a small bowl. Set aside.

To make the omelette, beat together the eggs, cream, salt, and pepper in a small bowl.

In a frying pan over high heat, warm the goose fat until hot. Add the mushrooms and sauté until soft, 1 to 2 minutes. Reduce the heat to low. Sprinkle half of the *persillade* over the mushrooms. Quickly pour in the egg mixture and, using a heatproof rubber spatula, gently stir to combine. As the eggs cook and begin to set along the edge, lift the set portions with the spatula and tilt the pan to one side to allow the uncooked egg to run underneath. Continue to cook until the omelette is set but still a bit moist, about 4 minutes.

Slide the omelette out of the pan onto a plate, using the spatula to fold the top half over the bottom. Sprinkle with the remaining *persillade* and serve right away.

MAKES 2 SERVINGS

For the *persillade*:

1 garlic clove, minced

2 tablespoons minced fresh parsley

For the omelette:

6 extra-large eggs

2 tablespoons (30 ml) heavy whipping cream

½ teaspoon coarse salt

¼ teaspoon pepper

2 tablespoons (29 g) goose fat or shortening

3 oz (90 g) fresh porcini mushrooms, brushed clean and sliced

Chilled White Asparagus
with Champagne Orange Sauce

Found in markets and on bistro menus all over France during its short season (April through June), white asparagus is lightly coated with a mustard vinaigrette and often sprinkled with chopped egg. We put our own zesty twist on the original.

———————————◆◆———————————

Prepare an ice bath in a mixing bowl large enough to hold the asparagus with 1 quart (1 liter) water and ice.

Prepare the asparagus by cutting or snapping off any tough stems. Using a vegetable peeler, scrape the asparagus from two-thirds of the way from the top to the bottom of the stalks to remove the tough outer skin. Tie into a bundle with string.

Bring water to a boil in a large stockpot. Cook the asparagus bundle in boiling water for 1 to 3 minutes, depending on the size of the asparagus. The asparagus is best served al dente. A fork should easily pierce the stalks but you should feel some resistance.

Remove the asparagus from the water and plunge into the ice bath. When the asparagus is chilled, about 30 seconds, remove from the bowl, remove the string, and chill until ready to serve.

To prepare the sauce, combine the vinegar, mustard, and egg yolks in a mixing bowl. Combine the olive and vegetable oils and add about 1 tablespoon at a time, whisking constantly until a mayonnaise-like consistency is formed. Stir in the orange juice concentrate, dill, salt, and hot sauce. Just before serving, add the Champagne.

To serve, place the asparagus on a platter in one vertical direction. Pour the sauce over the midsection of the stems and allow the sauce to pool on the platter.

MAKES 4 SERVINGS

1 pound (500 g) fresh white asparagus

2 tablespoons (30 ml) white
wine vinegar

2 tablespoons Dijon mustard

2 extra-large egg yolks

½ cup (250 ml) olive oil

½ cup (250 ml) vegetable oil

2 tablespoons orange juice concentrate

1 tablespoon chopped fresh dill

½ teaspoon coarse salt

½ teaspoon (2.5 ml) bottled hot sauce

⅓ cup (80 ml) Champagne

Roasted Eggplant, Tomato, and Cheese Tart

Eggplants and tomatoes plucked straight from the market are roasted to enhance the flavor of this savory tart. You may substitute zucchini, mushrooms, peppers, or leeks for the eggplants and tomatoes, and add some of Benoit's ham for extra flavor. No matter what filling you choose, the tart is perfect Dordogne picnic fare.

MAKES 4 TO 6 SERVINGS

2 medium eggplants

Coarse salt

4 large tomatoes, cut into 1-inch-thick (2.5-cm) slices

¼ cup (60 ml) olive oil, divided

Cracked pepper

3 extra-large eggs

2 cups (500 ml) heavy whipping cream

¼ pound (125 g) goat cheese

⅛ teaspoon ground nutmeg

1½ cups (6 oz/170 g) shredded Swiss cheese

1 9-inch (23-cm) packaged pie shell, baked according to package instructions

2 tablespoons chopped fresh basil

1 tablespoon chopped fresh chives

Preheat the oven to 300°F (150°C).

Peel the eggplants and cut into 1-inch-thick (2.5-cm) slices. Lay flat on paper towels, sprinkle with salt, and let stand for 20 minutes.

Meanwhile, arrange the tomato slices in a single layer on a baking sheet. Drizzle with 2 tablespoons of the oil and season with salt and pepper. Roast until the tomatoes begin to soften, about 30 minutes. Let cool to room temperature.

Blot the eggplant slices dry and arrange in a single layer on a baking sheet. Drizzle with the remaining oil and season with salt and pepper. Roast until the eggplant is soft but the slices still retain their shape, about 40 minutes. Let cool to room temperature.

Raise the oven temperature to 350°F (180°C).

In a medium bowl, mix together the eggs, cream, and goat cheese. Season with the nutmeg and salt and pepper. Sprinkle the Swiss cheese into the pie shell and arrange the roasted eggplant and tomato slices on top. Pour the egg mixture over the top and sprinkle with the basil and chives. Bake until the tart is set, 35 to 40 minutes.

Slice and serve warm or at room temperature.

Roast Chicken with
Truffle Butter and Monbazillac

Standing out in the cold and rain at the Issigeac market, we dreamed up this version of roast chicken. Dressed with a noble cloak of earthy truffles and the region's finest sweet wine, the humble bird becomes a festive dish with a *Périgord* twist.

Preheat the oven to 375°F (190°C).

Rinse the chicken, pat dry with paper towels, and place in a large roasting pan.

In a small bowl, combine 4 tablespoons of the butter, the truffle oil, 1 teaspoon salt, and ½ teaspoon pepper.

Using a vegetable peeler or a very sharp paring knife, cut the truffle into paper-thin slices.

Gently slide your fingers under the skin of the chicken, starting at the breast and working towards the thigh, and loosen it away from the flesh. Slip the truffle butter under the skin and spread it around as evenly as possible. Slip the sliced truffles on top of the butter and press the skin back into place. Rub the remaining 2 tablespoons butter over the outside of the chicken and season with salt and pepper. Combine the wine and lemon juice and pour over the chicken. Add the onions to the pan.

Roast the chicken for 15 minutes. Reduce the oven temperature to 350°F (180°C) and baste the chicken with the pan juices. Continue to roast until the chicken is golden and a thermometer inserted into the thickest part of the thigh registers 180°F (82°C), about 1 hour and 15 minutes.

Let the chicken rest for 10 minutes before carving.

MAKES 4 SERVINGS

1 whole roasting chicken
(7 to 8 lb/3.5 to 4 kg)

6 tablespoons (90 g) unsalted butter,
softened, divided

1 tablespoon truffle oil (15 ml)

Coarse salt and cracked pepper

1 small black truffle

1 cup (250 ml) Monbazillac or
other white dessert wine

2 tablespoons (30 ml) lemon juice,
freshly squeezed

1 pound (500 kg) small boiling
onions, peeled

Canelés

Rarely seen in the United States, these little cakes are becoming ubiquitous in France. Originally from the Bordeaux region, *canelés* have made their way east to Dordogne markets and make a delightful companion to coffee and tea. Their crunchy, caramelized shell and creamy heart of vanilla and rum are irresistible. Traditionally, they are made in small, specially shaped molds, but any mini fluted baking pan or silicone mold will do. The batter is made over several days, so be sure to plan ahead.

———————————————— •◆• ————————————————

In a saucepan over medium heat, add the milk. Scrape in the seeds from the vanilla bean and add the bean. Warm until small bubbles appear along the edge of the pan. Remove from the heat and let cool completely. Cover and refrigerate overnight. Remove the vanilla bean before using.

In a large bowl, whisk together the melted butter, eggs, and sugar until blended. Add the flour and vanilla milk and continue whisking until smooth. Stir in the rum, orange zest, and salt. Cover and refrigerate for 24 to 48 hours.

Using a pastry brush, heavily brush room-temperature butter over 12 to 16 *canelé* molds or other mini fluted baking pans, carefully buttering every ridge. Chill the molds until the butter is set.

Preheat the oven to 450°F (230°C).

Whisk the chilled batter until smooth and ladle into the molds, filling each about three-fourths full. Bake until the tops are caramelized, about 45 minutes. Immediately unmold the *canelés* onto a cooling rack or, if using silicone molds, wait 10 minutes before unmolding. Serve warm or at room temperature.

MAKES 12 TO 16 SERVINGS

2 cups (500 ml) whole milk

1 vanilla bean, split lengthwise

3 tablespoons (43 g) unsalted butter, melted

3 large eggs

½ cup (125 g) sugar

¾ cup (100 g) all-purpose flour

3 tablespoons (45 ml) dark rum

1 teaspoon orange zest

⅛ teaspoon salt

Chapter 3

The Royal Families

FOR most amateur wine enthusiasts like us, French wine means bordeaux or champagne, a rich burgundy or refreshing rosé from Bandol in the heat of summer, so it was a pleasant surprise to discover the Dordogne not only dishes up some great meals, but also produces some outstanding wines and spirits to accompany them. The vineyards of the Dordogne are heavily concentrated around Bergerac and produce thirteen different Appelation d'origine contrôlée wines, and discovering all the wine of the region could take years. Among the most well-known are those of Bergerac, Rosette, Montravel, Saussignac, Pécharmant, and the famous Monbazillac wine, from the region whose noble castle is as recognizable as the famed white wine it produces.

The Château at Monbazillac is a must for any lover of architecture. Encircled by a moat, two bridges, and six thousand acres of vines, the castle was spared the ravages of wars that have ransacked other landmarks, and shows off a distinct medieval and Renaissance style. We love history like the next guy, but let's be honest . . . we really showed up for the wine! The sweet treat is something to behold and is as synonymous with regional cuisine as foie gras. It's no wonder the two remain loyal companions on menus around the Dordogne. For a real summertime splash, our friend Sally served Monbazillac over fresh melon as a cool and refreshing *entrée*.

The regal château de Monbazillac

The wine is a concentrated sweet wine, similar to a sauterne, perfected by the naturally occurring botrytis, or "noble rot." The misty mornings and sunny afternoons create the perfect stage for this ripening process that results in a sweet, honey-colored wine worth stocking in your own cellars. We bought a few cases and have enjoyed them as aperitifs in the evening, served with foie gras or over melon, and we have even served it with dessert (heck, even *as* dessert) from time to time.

The Château de Monbazillac is found along the Route des Vins (Wine Route), along which more than one hundred estates, large and small, invite you in to meet the growers and sample the wines. The burgundy-colored signs with grape symbol are ubiquitous, and we spent days, it seems (or maybe that was just the wine talking), driving up and down roads just big enough for one and a half French-sized cars, flanked by undulating hills carpeted with green vines.

There are actually four different circuits to follow, ranging from fifty to ninety-five miles long. Some lead you to tasting rooms in grand Renaissance châteaux, like the one at Monbazillac, while others guide you down less-traveled roads to family homes, like that of the charming Dubard vineyards in Saint-Méard-de-Gurçon, where a dog ran along the pathway, barking our arrival, and a bicycle leaned against a wooden post. We wondered if we shouldn't have come by bike ourselves. We knocked and knocked, but no one answered. Eventually, the bellowing dog brought with him a man (presumably the neighbor, but we actually have no idea where he came from), who informed us that the family was *en congé* (off work), and we should come back after the weekend. Little did he know we actually had no idea where we were. We realized then that what we really enjoyed most about the Dordogne, and the wine route in particular (aside from the wine, of course), were the serendipitous possibilities. Hidden villages, vineyards, and flavors we may not have found otherwise and possibly (likely) could never find again

were set out before us. The undisciplined direction of the road was the charm, and for two people who usually live by schedules and agendas, this was liberating.

Like food, wine is subjective, and the beauty is in the glass of the beholder. We won't presume to tell you which one is best—we are not experts—but we have thoroughly enjoyed exploring the vineyards of the Pécharmant region located east of Bergerac and north of the Dordogne River. The Pécharmant wine has been a classified AOC since 1936 and draws its distinct taste from the sand-and-gravel soil. Like we said, we're not wine experts, and though we like to find good products, what we seek is a better understanding of those who call the Dordogne home. Behind many of these doors are winemakers whose passion and perseverance are buried deep in the ground here, and whose products reflect a respect for family and patrimony that goes deeper than we will ever understand. Our first visit to the tiny *Domaine du Haut-Pecharmant* revealed five generations of family living and working together to sustain the legacy created by a matriarch back in a time when running a vineyard was a man's job. We were rendered silent (something difficult to accomplish) at the sight of a young brother pushing his sister in a swing, set up among the vines, while Madame Roches, her son, and grandsons looked on. Their obvious love and admiration for one another and their work was more intoxicating than any wine itself. If only we could have bottled that to bring home to America.

Not far from here is the stately manor home of Château de Tiregand, where we met the charming François Xavier de Saint Exupéry, a descendent of the famous author Antoine, whose masterpiece *The Little Prince* made famous the Saint Exupéry name. François and his wife, Monique, generously offered us a tour of the family home (not open to the public), and after a few hours spent with this passionate wine family, we are convinced the Saint Exupéry name will be linked not only with a little prince, but also with fine Pécharmant wine.

Our philosophy on good wine is really quite simple. If served hand in hand with good food and celebration, there is nothing finer. Our only advice to you is, drink what you like, serve it with a delicious meal, and enjoy it in the company of good friends. We have had the pleasure of meeting, dining, and sharing a glass or two with countless friends in the Dordogne, and with vintners whose families have been creating wine for centuries. For us, this has made the wines of the Dordogne all the sweeter.

EVEN if you are not a liquor lover, this distillery, which prides itself on tradition and has been in the same family since 1905, merits a visit. Louis Roque set up shop in the small town of Souillac, not far from the stunning village of Rocamadour (of goat cheese fame), and soon became a specialist in liquors and brandies, most notably a plum brandy called La Vieille Prune (recipe top secret, we are told), considered to be the crème de la crème of liquors. Louis Roque's grandson André Bizac now runs the business, and the repertoire of flavors has expanded to include pear, raspberry, and truffle brandies, as well as popular liqueur flavors, like walnut. We have used many a drop of their walnut elixir to liven the flavors of salads and desserts.

On a rainy Tuesday, we were the only visitors, and we were greeted warmly by the charming Jessica, who has worked with the family for a few years. The tour started in the main lobby, which was more like a museum, but it was back behind the wooden doors where things got more interesting. The Louis Roque liquor is aged in ancient oak casks, and each of the one hundred thousand bottles per year is corked and labeled by hand. Intriguing were the bubbling cauldrons of green, red, blue, and yellow liquids that splattered all over a workbench. Jessica revealed this to be the wax that seals each and every bottle, also done entirely by hand. The tour was short, and it ended in the labeling room, where two others wet and stick, wet and stick, wet and stick labels all day long. There was a tasting, of course, and we sampled the famed La Vielle Prune brandy as well as the walnut wine, and even sampled some strange flavors, like truffle and juniper berry. It's an acquired taste, but we left with several bottles of the liquor that has put this small, family-run distillery on the menus of some of France's best restaurants. Now, that's a tradition worth raising a glass to. ■

Bottles are sealed by hand with colorful wax.

"I wanted to come back to my roots."

IN *THE LITTLE PRINCE*, Antoine de Saint Exupéry wrote, "Here is my secret. It is very simple. It is only with the heart that one can see rightly; what is essential is invisible to the eye." It is an oft-used quotation, probably because it is relevant and applicable to so many things: love, friendship, and, in this case, wine. While the writing of Antoine brought his name worldwide fame in 1943, the Saint Exupéry family has been quietly making a name for itself among the vines of the Dordogne for more than three hundred years.

We first discovered the Château de Tiregand in Creysse when we followed a small, hard-to-see sign off the D660 and bounced along a dusty road. We bottomed out our rental car, but it was worth it. Since then the road has improved some, and we have brought dozens of friends and culinary tour guests back to taste the delicious wines and to meet the charming prince of an owner, François-Xavier de Saint Exupéry and his wife, Monique.

Today, François greets us in a suit and looks as if he has been in the boardroom and not the barrel room. Discussing wine is obviously serious business for this soft-spoken family man. He has just finished tasting his wines with an enologist, something he does once a month and says is always a learning experience; "We discuss what we like, what we don't like, and each time, you teach yourself."

As we walk through the barrel room with François, he continues: "Pécharmant has a distinct taste because of the soil here. Tasting teaches me about quality, and in doing so, I hope to produce an elegant Pécharmant wine. A better wine."

We see the remnants of a tasting in the château's ancient kitchen, where an old pot called a *peyrol* still stands in the oversize stone fireplace, and a half dozen empty bottles of Pétrus, Cheval Blanc, and

Château Margaux bear witness to what looks like a great party. "Knowing other wines is also part of the learning process," he says, "And understanding what is good and bad about other wines helps improve your own."

The Château de Tiregand has been in the Saint Exupéry family for four generations and is currently run by a small team of twelve, including François. He was one of eleven children and learned the business young, from his father. At the age of twenty-eight, François moved to California's Napa Valley, where he worked in and visited innumerable wineries during a six-month period. He tasted, compared, and most important, learned. He smiles remembering his days in the famed wine region. "I had quite the life," he admits. "I would work from seven in the morning until three, then golf in the afternoon every day."

His favorite local wines were those of the Francis Ford Coppola winery and Heitz Cellars. François was offered a chance to produce his own wine in California, but the family pull was too strong, "I wanted to come back to my roots, and the pride I had for my family heritage brought me the desire to develop something here at home."

Looking around the eleven hundred acres of vines that are imprinted with the footprints of family history, it's not hard to imagine why. For François, it was a calling. His destiny, he says, but he doesn't know what's in store for his own children. He says he'd love his three sons to follow in his footsteps, but only if they really want to. "I tell my sons, 'Do your own thing, but do it with desire.'" At a minimum, François is sure that whatever they do, they will still take with them an essential element. "I believe the love of good food and good wine is a gift you give your children to last their whole life."

Sharing the gift of good food and wine is evident in all they do. Monique is often seen pouring wine for visitors,

and she tells us she is also the family cook. Large family meals are de rigueur, and the local restaurateurs come to the château annually for a wine-tasting dinner, which she also prepares herself. "I like to cook fish and lamb to change things a bit from the typical duck dishes."

The château is a regal manor house belonging to the heirs of the countess François de Saint Exupéry but is now the family home. It is not open to the general public, but François graciously invites us in and guides us through some of the rooms, the old kitchen, and the gardens. As we crunch around the gravel path, we feel as if we are turning the pages of a family photo album. François points to various spots. "Here is where we had the wedding dinner of my nephew," he says as we pass a large terrace. Pointing to a grassy area boxed in with colorful flower beds, he says, "Here is a wonderful place for children to play, and here," he continues, spreading his arms open as we come to rest near the château doors, "is a place that gets cool shadows in the summer and is an excellent place to serve an aperitif."

In France, food is a topic of discussion 24/7, much like the weather is for old people, so we are not surprised when François begins pouring wine while suggesting various meals we might enjoy with each. We try a rosé that François recommends with a light lunch on a sunny terrace. We follow it with a white wine that is crisp and refreshing. Monique suggests an accompanying meal of fish or eel from the Dordogne River. We finish off with a rich red, vintage 1985. François is too entranced to recommend a meal. He's clearly gone elsewhere.

Holding the stem of his wineglass, François closes his eyes and tilts it towards his nose. He inhales deeply and takes in the scent of the wine that is a blend of his heritage, his passion, and his future. The taste is apparently sublime. Like Antoine de Saint Exupéry, we, too, have a secret. François, this descendant of a little prince, has found what is essential, and it's right before his eyes. ■

A QUEEN

TRYING TO FIND this place the first time was difficult, and on try number two, after a few roundabouts and a missed sign, we were completely lost. Luckily for us, a shop owner knew of Reine Roches and exactly how to find her family's vineyard, Domaine du Haut Pécharmant. As we soon learned, he was not the only one.

Reine, the word for queen in French and her real name, was destined to live up to her noble moniker. She grew up among the grapes of the Pécharmant region and has been nurturing these fields and her family for the better part of eighty years. Not only has she created an impressive array of wines, but also a thriving family business and a reputation that precedes her. "She's famous," says Olivier when he introduces his eighty-five-year-old grandmother as "Madame Roches." He adds, "You can't escape the history."

Looking less like a family matriarch and more like a proud grandmother, Reine squeezes Olivier's arm and smiles, moving slowly with her walking stick to greet us. Olivier and his brother, Didier, are the fourth generation to manage the business and are unmistakably proud to be a part of this living history. Michel Roches, Reine's son and Olivier and Didier's father, joins us in the wine cave for a short tour.

"We have always been aware of the presence of those who have been here before us," reflects Michel. "My mother transferred to me a magnificent job, and all I had to do was follow her example. Now, my sons take part in this story." The story to which he refers is one that links Michel to his past and an inspiring one for the generations that follow. Reine was born just across the dirt path from where we now stand, on the land the family calls Domaine de Peyrelevade. Seven years later, her father sold it to buy the current plot, Domaine du Haut

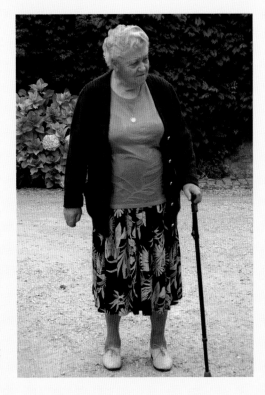

"We have always worked the land here, and these are my fields."

Pécharmant. Reine recalls, "We didn't have far to move. We loaded up our carts and crossed the path."

While there were vines on the land, Reine says her father originally made his living raising dairy cows and growing wheat. Any grapes produced were sold in bulk to wineries in Bergerac. As the oldest child, Reine dropped out of school at age thirteen to help her father with the farm. She did everything from taking care of the livestock to planting the vines and tilling the fields, and, of course, she tasted a little wine along the way. When she married a winemaker from Saint Laurent, the couple took over the property. Everything was going well, she says, until her husband suddenly passed away. Reine recalls that many in the business didn't think she would succeed on her own and predicted she would sell the land. What these naysayers didn't count on was Reine's courage and determination to preserve her family name.

"My roots were here," says Reine. "We have always worked the land here, and these were my fields." With advice from family friends, Reine sold her cows, turned the barn into a wine shed, and constructed eight wine vats. Remembering everything her father had taught her, Reine produced the first large wine production under her own label, Domaine du Haut Pécharmant, in 1978. She was the winemaker until 1983, when Michel took over the reigns.

Today the Domaine du Haut Pécharmant is receiving a lot of recognition. Their wines recently won a medal at a competition in Paris, and Olivier says it has helped that wine bars have become trendy in large cities around the world, prompting curiosity about smaller vineyards like theirs. "It's good for your health too," he jokes, "so we should all drink more."

The winery produces 150,000 bottles per year, selling mostly within the region and Europe, and has developed a reputation synonymous with quality and local patrimony. Reine recalls local restaurateurs insisting, "If there is a Veuve Cliquot, then we must have our Veuve Roches." (*Veuve* means widow in French.) Michel obliged. In 1985 and every year since, there has been a special Veuve Roches *cuvée*. "It's the least I could do for her," he says. There are also wines named after each of Reine's great-grandchildren, including the most recent, Jolie Julie, which means "pretty Julie."

In the reception room visitors come and go, and Reine greets them with welcoming eyes that express an insatiable passion and pride. She serves us a small plate of cheese and crackers and lights up when we ask her about cooking for her family. Reine grew up in the kitchen and learned to cook at her grandmother's knee. She has prepared limitless meals, from intimate family birthdays to large harvest dinners. Without hesitation, she recites by heart a recipe for *pintade* (guinea hen) stuffed with grapes. Olivier reminds her of a wine-tasting dinner that ended with whipped cream flying around the room, and they both laugh at the memory.

Looking around the modest buildings and garden hidden among these eighty-two acres of vibrant vines, we get a true appreciation for what this place really is. It's more than a family business; it's the business of family. "It's a hard life and demands an enormous amount of time," Olivier says, "but yes, it's a life I love. I never wanted to do anything else. Not at all."

Young Julie appears out of nowhere, running down a dirt path with her brother and a barking, black dog on their heels. Stopping at the picnic table where Reine is now seated, the young boy kisses his great-grandmother on the cheek, then dashes off to push his sister back and forth on the swing that is set up outside the tasting room. Olivier walks up to the table, and Michel soon joins his family. "The fifth generation," Olivier says, nodding toward his children on the swing.

With a queen as their guide, and with history rooted deep in the soil and vines, this is just the beginning for this royal family. ∎

Chilled Cantaloupe with Monbazillac

Our friend Sally used to live among the vineyards of Monbazillac, just South of Bergerac, and she served us this simple and refreshing entrée at her historic home Le Prieuré in Biron. The wine's rich tones of honey and peach combine with ripe melon for a simple and elegant beginning to any feast.

MAKES 4 SERVINGS

1 ripe cantaloupe

½ cup (125 ml) Monbazillac or other white dessert wine

4 sprigs fresh mint or other green herb, for garnish

Have ready four 6-ounce (180-ml) coupe glasses.

Halve the cantaloupe and scoop out and discard the seeds. Cut the flesh into 1-inch (2.5-cm) cubes. Divide the cantaloupe among the glasses. Pour the wine over the cantaloupe, dividing it evenly. Chill for about 30 minutes.

Garnish each glass with a sprig of fresh mint and serve right away.

Monique's Pan-Roasted Leg of Lamb with Crown of Garlic Confit

At Château de Tiregand, we asked Monique to share a family recipe with us. She says she often chooses lamb for her special occasion dinners in lieu of the typical duck dishes. This one is a real crowd pleaser.

◆◆◆

Preheat the oven to 350°F (180°C).

Trim the excess fat and sinewy tissue from the lamb and season the meat well with salt and pepper.

In a large, heavy frying pan over medium-high heat, warm the goose fat until just smoking. Add the lamb and sear, turning to brown all sides. Reduce the heat to medium.

Pour the Armagnac over the lamb and cook until the Armagnac boils off. Transfer the lamb to a roasting pan and set aside.

Add the garlic cloves to the frying pan and stir to coat with the pan juices. Add the wine and cook for about 1 minute. Transfer the garlic and pan juices to a baking dish with a tight-fitting lid. Bake until tender but not mushy, about 1 hour.

Pour the stock into the roasting pan with the lamb and roast for 35 minutes. Do not cover the lamb or baste while cooking. Add the garlic and pan juices to the roasting pan with the lamb and continue to roast until the meat reaches an internal temperature of 145°F (63°C) for medium rare, 10 to 25 more minutes.

Let the lamb rest for 10 to 15 minutes before serving. Transfer the lamb to a large carving platter and spoon the garlic confit around it to create a "crown." Taste the pan juices and add a little water, if necessary, to make a sauce to serve on the side.

MAKES 6 SERVINGS

1 bone-in leg of lamb
(5 to 6 lb/2.5 to 3 kg)

Coarse salt and cracked pepper

3 tablespoons (43 g) goose fat
or butter

½ cup (125 ml) Armagnac

80 to 100 garlic cloves
(4 to 5 heads), peeled

1 cup (250 ml) Monbazillac wine or
other white dessert wine

1 cup (250 ml) beef or veal stock

Seared Duck Breast
with Walnuts and Raspberries

For five generations, Louis Roque has been distilling the abundant walnuts of the Dordogne into an addictive elixir called La Vieille Noix. The fine liqueur, tart raspberries, and walnuts marry for a beautiful and elegant pan sauce for seared duck breast.

———————◆◆◆———————

MAKES 4 SERVINGS

2 duck breasts, preferably *magret* (⅓ to ½ lb/155 to 250 g each)

Coarse salt and cracked pepper

2 tablespoons (30 ml) Armagnac

2 tablespoons (30 ml) walnut liqueur, preferably La Vieille Noix

2 tablespoons (30 ml) demi-glace

1 cup (125 g) fresh raspberries

½ cup (60 g) walnut halves, toasted

With a sharp knife, trim any excess fat from the edge of each duck breast. Score the fat on the top of each breast at 2-inch (5-cm) intervals in a crisscross pattern, being careful not to cut into the flesh. Season with salt and pepper.

Place the duck breasts, skin side down, in a heavy frying pan over medium heat. Cook, uncovered, until the skin begins to brown, 5 to 8 minutes. Reduce the heat and continue to cook until the skin is brown and begins to crisp, about 5 minutes longer. Turn the breasts over and cook until crisp, 3 to 4 minutes longer. Transfer the duck breasts to a plate and pour off all but 1 tablespoon of the duck fat from the frying pan.

Return the pan to medium heat and add the Armagnac and walnut liqueur; be careful as the pan may flame up. Deglaze the pan, using a spatula to loosen any browned bits from the bottom. Add the demi-glace and raspberries and cook for 30 seconds. Add the walnuts and stir until heated through, about 30 seconds. Do not overcook the sauce; the raspberries should hold their shape.

Starting at the smaller end, thinly slice the duck breast at a 45-degree angle. Arrange the slices on four serving plates and spoon the sauce on top.

Fingerling Potatoes
with Cèpes and Shallots

Autumn in the Dordogne means the world-famous *cèpes* (porcini mushrooms) market in Monpazier and Villefranche-du-Perigord where literally tons of the woodsy delicacies are sold. Made with potatoes and cream, this rich side dish complements a hearty meat dish like Monique's roasted lamb (page 93) and goes especially well with a fine bottle of Château de Tiregand's Pécharmant wine.

⸻ ●● ⸻

Fill a large stockpot three-fourths full with salted water and bring to a boil over high heat. Add the potatoes and cook until just tender, about 10 minutes. Drain the potatoes and transfer to a bowl of ice water to cool. When cool enough to handle, halve the potatoes lengthwise.

In a frying pan over medium-high heat, melt the butter. Add the shallots and sauté until tender, about 2 minutes. Add the mushrooms and sauté until the mushrooms are tender, about 5 minutes. Add the potatoes to the pan and sauté until heated through, about 3 to 4 minutes. Add the cream and simmer until it is bubbly and thickens slightly, about 8 minutes.

Season with salt and pepper, sprinkle with the parsley, and serve right away.

MAKES 6 SERVINGS

2 pounds (1 kg) fingerling potatoes

4 tablespoons (60 g) unsalted butter

4 shallots, sliced

8 oz (250 g) porcini mushrooms, brushed clean, stemmed, and julienned

1 cup (250 ml) heavy whipping cream

Coarse salt and cracked pepper

¼ cup (15 g) chopped fresh parsley

Reine Roches' Pintade

Madame Roches, the matriarch of the five-generation-young Domaine du Haut Pécharmant wine estate, twinkled when we asked for her recipe for roast *pintade* (guinea hen) with a bread stuffing dipped in the bird's blood, a birthday dinner tradition in her family. We took a little liberty with her recipe, dipping the bread in red wine instead. We hope the result makes Madame Roches proud.

Preheat the oven to 375°F (190°C).

In a small bowl, soak the porcini mushrooms in the warm water until softened, about 15 minutes. Strain the mushrooms, reserving the liquid.

Rinse the hen, pat dry with paper towels, and place in a large roasting pan.

In a frying pan over medium-high heat, melt 2 tablespoons of the butter. Add the shallots, season lightly with salt and pepper, and sauté until the shallots are soft and beginning to color, about 2 minutes. Transfer to a bowl.

Return the frying pan to the heat and add 2 more tablespoons of the butter. When the butter is melted, add the shiitake mushrooms and season lightly with salt and pepper. Roughly chop the porcini mushrooms, if necessary, and add to the pan. Cook for about 1 minute longer. Transfer the mushrooms to the bowl with the shallots.

Return the frying pan to the heat. Add 2 cups (500 ml) of the wine and deglaze the pan using a spatula to loosen any browned bits from the bottom of the pan. Bring the wine to a boil, remove from the heat, and add 2 tablespoons of the butter and the demi-glace. Transfer the sauce to a shallow bowl.

Stir the dried thyme into the shallot-mushroom mixture. Remove 2 to 3 tablespoons of the mixture and place in a separate bowl. Add 4 tablespoons of the butter to the bowl, mix well to combine, and set aside.

Dip the bread slices into the wine sauce and stuff a few slices into the cavity of the hen, followed by some of the shallot-mushroom mixture. Continue stuffing the hen, alternating between the bread and the shallot-mushroom mixture, until you have used all of the bread and the mixture.

MAKES 4 SERVINGS

6 ounces (170 g) dried porcini mushrooms

½ cup (125 ml) warm water (120°F/49°C)

1 guinea hen, 1 roasting chicken, or 4 Cornish game hens (4 to 5 lb/2 to 2.5 kg total)

1½ sticks (185 g) unsalted butter, divided

12 shallots, chopped

Coarse salt and cracked pepper

1 pound (500 g) shiitake mushrooms, brushed clean and chopped

3 cups (750 ml) Pécharmant or red Bordeaux wine, divided

1 teaspoon (15 ml) demi-glace or good-quality beef flavoring

1 teaspoon dried thyme

10 to 12 slices day-old baguette, each about 1 inch (2.5 cm) thick

6 dried bay leaves

1 pound (500 g) purple table grapes, such as Ribier, halved and seeded

3 ripe fresh figs

Sprigs of fresh thyme, for garnish (optional)

Using your fingers, lightly loosen the skin over the breast and spread the reserved shallot-mushroom butter evenly between the skin and the meat. Rub the remaining 2 tablespoons butter on the outside of the skin and season with salt and pepper. Combine the remaining wine sauce and enough water to make 1 cup (250 ml) of liquid and pour into the roasting pan with the hen. Add the bay leaves and roast the hen for 20 minutes.

Add the remaining 1 cup (250 ml) wine, the grapes, and figs to the roasting pan and stir to coat with the pan juices. Season lightly with salt and pepper. Reduce the heat to 350°F (180°C) and continue roasting until a meat thermometer inserted into the breast reads 160°F (70°C), about 30 minutes longer.

Cover loosely with aluminum foil and let rest for 10 minutes before carving. Spoon some of the stuffing into the center of each dinner plate and arrange slices of the roast hen on top. Spoon some of the pan juices over each plate. Garnish with fresh thyme, if desired, and serve.

Sandrine's Duchesse de Sarlat

This cake with the regal name may not have its roots dating back to ancient Périgord, but it does have its fans here in the Dordogne. Our friends Sandrine and Eric Miane at the *Ferme Aubuerge* Maraval in Cénec-et-Saint-Julien provided us with this recipe for their version of a creamy cake made with ladyfingers and home-grown walnuts.

Mix together the walnuts, 1¼ cups of the confectioners' sugar, and the butter until very soft and creamy. Set aside.

Pour milk into a saucepan. Split the vanilla bean and scrape the seeds into the milk; then gently heat over a medium flame, being careful not to boil or burn the milk. Combine the egg yolks, the remaining ¼ cup confectioners' sugar, and the flour and add to the milk mixture. Cook a few more minutes, stirring continuously to integrate all the ingredients, being careful not to let it burn or boil. Remove the pan from the heat and let cool to room temperature. Stir in the walnut mixture to create a thick cream.

Carefully arrange the ladyfingers upright around the sides and flat on the bottom of a rectangular baking dish or cake pan. Pour the cream mixture into the pan and cover the top with more ladyfingers. Cover with plastic wrap and refrigerate for at least 4 to 5 hours to allow the cream to set. This dessert can be made up to 24 hours in advance. Cut into squares and serve.

MAKES 4 SERVINGS

1½ cups (150 g) walnuts, grated

1½ cups (220 g) confectioners' sugar, divided

10 tablespoons (150 g) butter, softened

1 vanilla bean, split lengthwise

⅓ cup (80 ml) milk

3 large egg yolks

3 large tablespoons (25 g) all-purpose flour

---

30 ladyfingers

Chapter 4

The Alchemists

I F you are not a believer in alchemy, then you have never visited the kitchens of the Dordogne. The wizards here don't wear cloaks and pointy hats. Instead they have exchanged them for toques and white coats, but they are still creating magic in their own bubbling cauldrons. Like any good alchemist, these chefs drop in a pinch of the essential ingredient and in a puff of smoke seemingly turn metal to gold (or goose fat into a divine delicacy, as the case may be here). While this description may seem more Harry Potter than Julia Child, in modern kitchens it is not that far-fetched. We've all heard of El Bulli, the Catalan restaurant that is open six months a year. Chef Ferran Adrià reserves the other six for creating and testing avant-garde recipes in his Barcelona laboratory. There is nothing nearly as over-the-top on the Dordogne culinary scene, but there is definitely something brewing in these traditionally conservative kitchens.

As is typical in most small French communities, the best source of information in the Dordogne is on the streets and, as they say, *de bouche à l'oreille* (from mouth to ear). The locals at the market, shop owners, and restaurateurs know everything from where to find the plumpest tomatoes to how to cook the two pounds of *magret* (duck breast) we just bought. We made countless new discoveries by simply asking, "What is your favorite [fill in the blank]?" But our favorite go-to gal for Dordogne

Local chefs create magic in the kitchens of the Dordogne.

dining trends is Sally Evans, owner of the historic Le Prieuré in Biron. On our last visit, she revealed her latest dining obsession—a restaurant in Issigeac called La Brucelière and its inventive young alchemist, er, chef.

In a hotel formerly run by his parents, Nicolas De Visch and his wife, Maffe, have opened a cutting-edge Dordogne restaurant where not a single piece of duck is served. *Quelle horreur*! But fear not—Nicolas is expert at marrying tradition with innovation; he uses local products and skillfully blends them with Asian influences. Judging from La Brucelière's packed terrace at lunchtime, his fusion of old and new seems to be well accepted. Nicholas's Dordogne River fish cooked in yellow Thai curry served with vegetables sauteed in sesame oil was one of the best local meals we have ever had, and the wasabi-potato foam dispensed from a gadget that looked like Nicolas was preparing to caulk a bathtub was delightfully reminiscent of El Bulli. In fact, we found his synthesis of flavors so magical we practically licked our plates clean (actually, one of us may have done this).

Upon seeing our delight for the unusual, Nicolas dashed to the kitchen and returned with a white plastic container and a smile. He insisted we taste something "sensational," as if we hadn't already! He

One of Nicolas De Visch's beautiful and tasty creations

THE château and suspended gardens of Marqueyssac in Vézac is a privately owned estate and nineteenth-century garden perched on a ridge above the Dordogne Valley, and a visit here might just convince you that fairy tales are real.

Our first trip to the gardens wasn't planned. On our way to another location, with "time to kill," we simply followed the sign. We figured we would wander around for twenty minutes, shoot some photos and leave. *Au contraire.* Looking at the manicured bushes and swirling rosemary garden, it was love at first site, and we decided to make a day of it.

Miles of paths took us through fifty-four acres of forested, sculptured, and flowering parkland dotted with an occasional waterfall and views to die for. From this elevated position you can pick your castle! Château de Beynac, Château de Feynac, and Château de Castelnaud were laid out before us at one end, and the riverside village of La Roque-Gageac was clearly visible from the other. The walking paths led us around the estate and to the belvedere, a balcony hanging 192 meters (nearly 630 feet) above the ground, with more exceptional views over the Dordogne River and its valley. Ultimately, the paths return to the estate's Château and an outdoor café that scoops out Roland Manouvrier's innovative ice cream and sorbet. We sat at the café, facing the distant Château de Beynac, and savored the flavor as well as the view.

We overheard a couple talking about Thursday evenings at Marqueyssac, when the paths are lit with tiny votive candles. We made plans to return and are glad we did. Though the views are obviously not as good in the dark, the twinkling candlelight cast a certain spell over the already enchanted gardens.

Like many of our adventures in the Dordogne, this spontaneous visit to Marqueyssac resulted in the discovery of one of our favorite locations. High above the Dordogne, we found something truly magical. ∎

handed us small espresso spoons and invited us to dig in to the tub of creamy, white ice cream. One by one we tasted, raising our eyebrows in delicious wonder. It was not coconut or vanilla or any other sweet flavor we had expected, but goat cheese ice cream made with *cabécou de Rocamadour*. Perhaps an acquired taste, but as we took another taste, we were intrigued.

Thanks to Nicolas, we hunted down the ice cream's creator, Roland Manouvrier, to find out what else he had up his sleeve. While Roland makes popular favorites like raspberry, strawberry, and cherry sorbet in his factory in Saint-Geniès, the real appeal of his concoctions is his unusual merging of flavors you might not normally consider for ice cream, let alone dessert. His flavors include a wide range, from Szechuan pepper, rosemary, or Parmesan, to a delicate, light-pink rose sorbet that tastes like a summer garden. Roland's creativity is limited only by his imagination, and perhaps a book of spells. We left, wondering how many times we'd have to visit La Brucelière for just one more taste. Fortunately, Roland's products, sold under the name Marco Polo, can be found at many locations around the region, including at the gardens of Marqueyssac and at the newly Michelin-star-stamped *L'Essentiel* in Perigueux. Thanks again to this word-of-mouth phenomenon, we met chef Eric Vidal, who serves Roland's classic ice cream flavors and justifies this with the smile of a little boy: "I serve what I like myself. I think ice cream should be sweet." Though classic in his approach, there is nothing ordinary about Eric's inventive menu. Aside from foie gras, we didn't find anything "ducky." We were surprised to see potatoes seasoned with five-spice powder, found in a lot of Asian dishes, and loved the new twist on typical Dordogne fare, like foie gras ravioli in truffle sauce, served as a side dish with pigeon. Eric's recommendation of the day—the seared tuna, served in a sauce of coconut and satay spice. Poof! The magicians are working their magic again.

Don't get us wrong—we love the culinary cornerstones that have given the region its gourmet gusto. Duck confit with *pommes sarladaise* is always our favorite comfort food, and truffles and foie gras will never go out of style. But for foodies who want to go beyond the boundaries of the typical Dordogne menu, we suggest you visit some of the area's new culinary magicians. Their creations are guaranteed to cast a spell over you.

Eric Vidal of *L'Essentiel*

THE DE VISCH DIFFERENCE

IN THE MEDIEVAL VILLAGE of Issigeac, a modern young chef patiently and meticulously creates his antidote to heavy Périgord cuisine. Armed with local products and a flair for Asian spice, La Brucelière's Nicolas De Visch is trying to sway devoted duck fans over to the lighter side.

When we arrive at the restaurant, an older couple checks out the menu outside the front door, then walks away. "That happens quite a bit," says Nicolas, who is waiting for us inside. "People are looking for duck, but we don't prepare it."

While some restaurant owners might fret over a lost customer, Nicolas and his wife, Maffe, understand that it's part of the slow process of informing—if not reforming—the traditional palates of the Périgord. Nicholas explains that he is not trying to supplant the old recipes, but rather to lighten up the duck-heavy Dordogne cuisine and bring something new and modern to the table—that takes some time in a region so deeply rooted in tradition. With a menu almost exclusively comprised of seafood pulled from the Dordogne River or brought in by suppliers in nearby Bordeaux, Nicolas certainly provides an alternative to the typical area restaurants. He has created a mouthwatering menu to tempt diehard duck lovers to trade in their feathers for fins. The blending of unconventional flavors and textures in dishes such as Savoy Cabbage, Salmon, and Lobster in Beurre Blanc is artistic alchemy. "For me, the important thing is to be different."

Different he is. And fast too. A whirling dervish in the kitchen, Nicolas ping-pongs between sizzling pans and a line-up of plates. We get tired just watching him juggle roasting pineapples, rolling cabbage, and whisking together a sauce destined for some lucky diner. We are curious when he brings out a gadget that could have easily been purchased at Home Depot rather than Williams-Sonoma. To our surprise, Nicolas takes aim at an all-white plate, paints on a swirl of pale green foam, then steps back to admire his handiwork. He hands us a plate to taste: wasabi and potato purée. Extraordinary!

Nicolas is no stranger to dishing up new surprises. In 1999, he began as the seafood chef at the luxurious Burj Al Arab hotel in Dubai (the one that looks like the giant sail). He was part of the opening team at this überchic Arabian palace, where he cooked out-of-this-world meals for superstars and royalty for almost four years. It is also where he met his wife, Maffe, who was working at the restaurant as a hostess. Life for the duo has changed a bit since they left Dubai in 2003 to pursue smaller kitchens and bigger dreams. The building that houses La Brucelière, along with a few guest rooms, once belonged to Nicolas's parents, who moved to the region more than fifty years ago. They were planning to sell the *chambre d'hôte* (bed-and-breakfast) right around the time when Nicolas and Maffe were looking for a change. They bought the building and began thinking about their future in the Dordogne. "We turned everything upside down and added a restaurant," said Nicolas. The couple now lives upstairs with their daughter and run the guesthouse and restaurant full-time.

On this busy Sunday, we are in the lobby and see no fewer than three separate groups turned away by an empathetic Maffe. She really does seem sorry to have to say no to people, but she lights up when she sees a familiar face. Sunday lunch is a favorite meal of the French, and the ever-popular market is going on today in Issigeac, which brings in a slew of regulars and newcomers in equal droves. Fortunately we were with our friend Sally, who booked our table on the terrace well in advance. In lieu of umbrellas, a large, white, billowing sail is spread out overhead to shield us from the summer sun, and we wonder if this unique touch is a reminder of Nicholas and Maffe's Dubai days. We see Maffe chatting with a table of four. She passes our table and places a soft hand on Sally's shoulder, as if to tell us she'll return soon. Meanwhile, Nicolas is a blur in the kitchen, stopping only to shift a piece of lobster one centimeter before it is whisked away and served to a salivating diner. He is soft-spoken, but his energy is palpable. The only thing he seems to slow down for is food, whether to introduce us to our next course, implore us to try a taste of some creative ice cream, or open a bottle of wine. He takes a brief break and pulls up chair to chat with us a bit, looking up at the blue sky past the edge of the white sail. As busy as it is, he says, he is happier because he is working for something personal now. "Everything we do is for us and our family. That's something I really wanted."

As far as we can see, life in the Dordogne agrees with Nicolas, and Nicolas agrees with the Dordogne. Two women stop by the table, and he rises to thank them for coming in. Based on their smiles and flamboyant hand gestures, we think they enjoyed the meal. Then Nicolas is on the go again. He waves at some new arrivals that have just been seated next to us and slowly pours a little more wine in our glass to make sure we enjoy the meal. "It's the people that really make the difference, isn't it?"

With Nicolas De Visch now firmly established in the culinary landscape of the Dordogne, we couldn't agree more. ∎

❧ THE TASTE OF SCENT ❧

IT HAS BEEN SAID that 75 percent of what we perceive as taste actually comes from our sense of smell. Scent is also linked to memory. To confirm this, one need only catch a whisper of a favorite perfume to be transported instantaneously to a particular moment in time. It is precisely this emotional voyage that has ice-cream maker Roland Manouvrier scheming up new flavors—appropriately enough called *parfums* in French—like foie gras and tomato-basil. "I like the idea of people responding to a specific flavor in an emotional or sensual way," he explains.

Roland met us wearing a lab coat and a large plastic cap set askew over his thick mop of dark hair. Looking very much the mad scientist, he greeted us with a handshake and a cone full of sweet, smooth, mandarin orange sorbet. It smelled and tasted as if we had plucked it straight from the tree. We looked around for smoking beakers and a bubbling cauldron, but all we saw was a spotless, stainless-steel kitchen.

A native of Saint-Léon-sur-Vézère, Roland attributes his connection to food to his mother and grandmother, who cooked "with local ingredients and a lot of emotion." He admires modern chefs who exploit the intelligent side of our palettes to create a sensory experience, referring to Ferran Adrià as an example. What intrigued us most about Roland was his attraction to the perfume makers of Paris in the Middle Ages, who created fragrances to provoke specific responses, such as falling in love. In his office, he identifies the brands of the perfume we are wearing, then asks if we have read Patrick Süskind's novel *Perfume*, in which the main character creates the ultimate scent, made from adolescent girls on the verge of womanhood. "I thought, why not adapt this concept to ice cream?" he says.

"To find the right balance between taste and texture is not exact. It is a reaction that depends on many influences."

There is no "essence of woman" flavor on Roland's menu (yet), but with each of his flavors he does strive to capture the true essence of his ingredients (often homegrown) so that it has impact far beyond the taste buds. His melding of color, scent, and texture is nothing short of alchemy, and he believes this sensory fusion is what lets people experience food, not just taste it. Roland uses only the freshest ingredients and regularly enjoys his own creations. His flavor preference may depend upon his mood or even the weather. This is part of the reason he doesn't write his recipes down. He explains, "To find the right balance between taste and texture is not exact. It is a reaction that depends on many influences." I guess we can't expect a magician to reveal *all* of his secrets.

We often forget the power of our senses, but here in Saint-Geniès, Roland is working hard to make sure we don't. His ability to conjure up flavor that tastes like fragrance is magical. That his creations look and feel as good as they taste is the icing, or shall we say the ice cream, on the cake. ∎

Roland's ice cream is a treat for all ages, but his speculoos flavor is a favorite of this young admirer.

Swirling rosemary in the gardens of Marqueyssac

Sandre and Scallops Scented with Grand Armagnac à la Truffe

The rivers of the Dordogne supply a delicate type of perch called *sandre* (zander), a favorite of some innovative local chefs. This recipe pairs *sandre* with scallops and a unique truffle-infused Armagnac in a perfect blend of the region's flavors. You can substitute perch or tilapia for the *sandre*. Serve with Eggplant Tian (page 122) for a beautiful main course.

Preheat the oven to 375°F (190°C).

Arrange the strips of fish on a work surface. Working with one strip of fish at a time, place a scallop close to one end of the strip and carefully wrap the fish around the scallop, forming a roll. Tie each roll with a chive or fasten with a toothpick.

In a large frying pan over medium-high heat, melt 2 tablespoons of the butter. Add the mushrooms and garlic and season lightly with salt and cayenne pepper. Sauté until the mushrooms begin to soften, 1 to 2 minutes. Transfer the mushrooms and pan juices to a small bowl.

Return the frying pan to the heat and add the remaining 2 tablespoons butter. When the butter is melted, arrange the fish-scallop rolls in the pan and season with salt and cayenne pepper. Cook until light golden brown, about 2 minutes. Turn the rolls over and add the Armagnac and lemon juice to the pan. Cook until the liquid is slightly reduced, about 1 minute. Add the cream and the mushrooms and their juices and cook until the sauce is slightly reduced, 6 to 8 minutes. Taste and adjust the seasonings with additional salt and cayenne pepper.

Sprinkle a small amount of parsley around the center of each plate. Arrange 4 fish-scallop rolls on each plate and spoon the sauce over the top. Serve right away.

MAKES 4 SERVINGS

1½ pounds (750 g) zander or perch filets, cut lengthwise into 16 strips

16 large fresh scallops

16 fresh chives or toothpicks

4 tablespoons (60 g) unsalted butter, divided

1 pound (500 g) shiitake mushrooms, brushed clean and sliced

1 garlic clove, minced

Coarse salt

Cayenne pepper

¼ cup (60 ml) Grand Armagnac à la Truffe (¼ cup Armagnac and 1 teaspoon black truffle oil)

2 tablespoons (30 ml) freshly squeezed lemon juice

1 cup (250 ml) heavy whipping cream

2 tablespoons chopped fresh parsley

Nicolas's Savoy Cabbage, Salmon, and Lobster in Beurre Blanc

One summer morning, we had the pleasure of preparing this delicately flavored dish with La Brucelière's Nicolas De Visch. Rolls of savoy cabbage and salmon are served alongside lobster and drizzled with a light butter sauce. Baby savoy cabbages may be found in specialty markets.

———————————●●———————————

Pick any bones from the salmon and cut the fillets on the bias into 3-inch medallions. Cover the medallions with plastic wrap, lightly flatten them, and refrigerate until ready to use.

Remove and discard the tough outer leaves from the baby cabbages. Flatten the spine of each cabbage with the back of a knife, trim the center core, and separate the leaves. Reserve the cabbage centers. If using a large cabbage, separate the leaves from the core; discard the core. Using scissors, cut thirty 4-inch (10-cm) circles from the leaves.

Fill a large stockpot three-fourths full with salted water and bring to a boil over high heat. Add the cabbage leaves and cook for about 30 seconds. With a slotted spoon, transfer the leaves to a bowl of ice water. Drain the leaves and place on a towel to dry. Repeat these steps with the snow peas, cabbage centers, and carrots, blanching them in batches. Cook the peas for about 30 seconds and the cabbage centers and carrots for about 2 minutes.

To assemble the cabbage-salmon rolls, start by placing a cabbage center or, if using a large cabbage, one of the circles rolled into a round ball on a work surface. Layer one piece of the salmon over the cabbage, then lay a cabbage leaf on top. Continue layering until you have used 3 salmon pieces and 4 cabbage leaves for each bundle. Cover each bundle with a piece of plastic wrap about 6 inches long. Carefully lift each bundle with the plastic wrap, twisting the plastic to form a round bundle that holds the salmon and cabbage together firmly. Cut off any excess plastic wrap. Place the rolls on a plate, twist side down, and refrigerate until ready to use.

MAKES 6 SERVINGS

1½ pounds (750 g) skinless salmon fillet

6 heads baby savoy cabbage or 1 head savoy cabbage

12 snow peas, trimmed

12 baby carrots

6 small lobster tails, cooked (about ¼ lb/125 g each)

For the beurre blanc:

2 shallots, minced

1 cup (250 ml) dry white wine

1 tablespoon white wine vinegar

1 pound (500 g) cold unsalted butter, cut into 1-inch (2.5-cm) cubes

Coarse salt and white pepper

6 sprigs fresh herbs of your choice, for garnish

Bring 1 inch of water to a boil in a pot. Place the rolls in a collapsible metal steamer basket. Set the basket in the pot, cover, and steam the rolls for 15 minutes. During the last few minutes of steaming, add the lobster tails and blanched pea pods and carrots and steam until heated through.

While the cabbage-salmon rolls are steaming, make the beurre blanc. In a saucepan over medium-high heat, combine the shallots, wine, and vinegar and bring to a boil. Simmer the sauce until reduced by half, 10 to 12 minutes. Reduce the heat to low.

Add the butter cubes, one at a time, and whisk until incorporated. Season with salt and white pepper. Keep the sauce warm until ready to use.

Remove the plastic wrap from a cabbage-salmon roll and arrange it on a serving plate with the round side facing upward. Place a lobster tail next to the roll. Spoon about 3 tablespoons of the beurre blanc over the cabbage-salmon roll, the lobster, and the plate. Garnish each plate with 2 snow peas, 2 carrots, and an herb sprig and serve right away.

Roasted Green Asparagus with Foie Gras and Truffle Vinaigrette

From the kitchen of Eric Vidal comes a modern Périgourdine dish that marries all the best traditions of the region with stellar flair. *L'Essentiel* in Perigueux earned its first Michelin star in 2008. We never had a doubt about the region's star potential and in our opinion, *L'Essentiel* shines brightest of all.

———————————— ◆❘◆❘◆ ————————————

Bring a large pot of water, big enough to hold the asparagus, to boil. Wash the asparagus and snap off any unusable ends. Add 16 of the asparagus spears to the boiling water and cook for 5 minutes. Remove from the boiling water and immediately plunge them into the bowl of ice water for 1 to 2 minutes; drain and set aside.

Melt the butter in a skillet over medium-high heat. Season the foie gras scallops with salt and pepper to taste. Cook the foie gras in the butter for 2 to 3 minutes (1 to 1½ minutes per side). Drain the foie gras and keep warm on a plate.

In a hot skillet over medium-high heat, roast the sixteen asparagus spears in the olive oil for about 2 minutes, or until heated through.

For the vinaigrette, combine the walnut oil, mustard, balsamic vinegar, and truffle and mix well.

Using a vegetable peeler, shave the remaining four asparagus spears into thin slivers.

To serve, place four cooked asparagus spears on each plate. Top the asparagus with a scallop of foie gras and some of the asparagus shavings. Sprinkle with the vinaigrette and serve.

MAKES 4 SERVINGS

20 large green asparagus spears

1 tablespoon butter

4 scallops of fresh foie gras, about 3.5 oz (100 g) each

Salt and pepper

2 tablespoons (30 ml) olive oil

6 tablespoons (90 ml) walnut oil

1 tablespoon whole-grain mustard

2 tablespoons (30 ml) balsamic vinegar

1 medium truffle, chopped

Eggplant Tian

The word *tian* refers to a shallow, clay baking dish, as well as to anything cooked in one. Though this attractive layered vegetable dish originated in Provence, it marries well with the fresh flavors of the Dordogne. It is the perfect accessory to fish dishes such as *Sandre* and Scallops Scented with Grand Armagnac à la Truffe (page 117), but it is equally satisfying grand served on its own as an *amuse-bouche* for an elegant lunch.

◆◆◆

Preheat the oven to 350°F (180°C). Have ready four 8-ounce (280-ml) ramekins.

Using a vegetable peeler, remove about half of the eggplant skin in 2-inch (5-cm) strips, leaving alternating strips of skin on the eggplant. Cut the eggplants, zucchini, and tomatoes crosswise into slices about ¾ inch (2 cm) thick. Arrange the vegetables on a baking sheet, brush with the oil, and sprinkle with salt and pepper. Bake until the vegetables are just soft, about 10 minutes.

In a small bowl, mix together the egg yolk, cream, and goat cheese until smooth. Season with salt and pepper.

Brush the bottom and sides of the ramekins with oil. Place a slice of roasted eggplant in the bottom of each ramekin and drizzle some of the goat cheese mixture on top. Continue layering, alternating between the zucchini, tomato, eggplant slices, and the goat cheese mixture and making at least 2 layers of each vegetable.

Bake until the *tian* are heated through and the goat cheese mixture is set, about 15 minutes. Let cool slightly. To unmold, center a serving plate on top of each ramekin, invert together, and gently lift off the ramekin. Run a thin, sharp knife around the edge of the ramekin to loosen the *tian*, if necessary. Sprinkle with chopped parsley and serve right away.

MAKES 4 SERVINGS

2 eggplants, each 4 inches (10 cm) in diameter

2 fresh zucchini, each 4 inches (10 cm) in diameter

4 large tomatoes, each 4 inches (10 cm) in diameter

¼ cup (60 ml) olive oil

Coarse salt and cracked pepper

1 extra-large egg yolk

2 tablespoons (30 ml) heavy whipping cream

3 tablespoons (45 g) fresh goat cheese

Fresh parsley, chopped, for garnish

Roland's Tomato-Basil Sorbet

"I don't write my recipes down, but for you—I will," said Roland Manouvrier with a laugh. We felt like quite the magicians getting this wizard to reveal his secret to the unexpected flavor and texture that makes this sorbet so bewitching.

Add the tomatoes and water to a large stockpot over low heat and bring to a simmer. Add the sugar and cook until the tomatoes are very soft, about 30 minutes. Pour the tomatoes and liquid into a nonreactive bowl, cover, and chill overnight.

In a food processor or blender, purée the tomatoes and liquid. Pour into a bowl and stir in the chopped basil and hot sauce. Freeze in an ice cream maker according to the manufacturer's directions.

Serve the sorbet softly frozen or freeze until firm, at least 3 hours. Serve two small scoops on each serving plate and garnish with basil leaves.

**MAKES ABOUT 1 QUART
(1 LITER)**

4 pounds (2 kg) ripe red tomatoes, cored, seeded, and chopped

3½ cups (875 ml) water

4 cups (1 kg) sugar

½ cup (30 g) chopped fresh basil leaves, plus whole leaves, for garnish

2 teaspoons (30 ml) hot pepper sauce

Lavender Crème Caramel
with Wild Strawberries

Described by a fellow diner as being "like having a bath and dessert at the same time," this sinfully good dessert fuses the flavors of freshly picked lavender and *fraises des bois*, the tiny, wild strawberries found in the woods.

———————————————•◦•———————————————

MAKES 6 SERVINGS

4 cups (1 liter) heavy whipping cream

½ cup fresh-cut lavender flowers

Pinch of coarse salt

1¾ cups (435 g) sugar, divided

8 extra-large egg yolks

1 cup (250 ml) whipped cream, for garnish (optional)

1 pint (250 g) small wild strawberries

Preheat the oven to 325°F (165°C). Have ready six 8-ounce (280-ml) ramekins and a large roasting pan.

In a heavy saucepan over medium-low heat, combine the heavy cream, lavender, and salt. Heat to just below a simmer and cook for 15 minutes. Remove from the heat and let steep uncovered for 1 hour, stirring occasionally. Pour the cream through a fine-mesh sieve; discard the lavender.

Meanwhile, heat 1 cup (250 g) of the sugar in a small, heavy saucepan over medium heat. Cook, stirring gently, until the sugar melts and is dark brown and caramelized, about 10 minutes. If necessary, remove the pan from the heat for a few seconds while stirring to avoid scorching. Pour the caramel into the ramekins, dividing it evenly among them. Quickly tilt the ramekins to cover the bottom and sides with the caramel.

In a small bowl, beat the egg yolks and the remaining ¾ cup (185 g) sugar until pale yellow. Spoon a small amount of the lavender cream into the egg yolk mixture and stir to dissolve the sugar. Pour the egg yolk mixture into the lavender cream and stir until completely blended and smooth.

Pour the custard into the prepared ramekins. Set the ramekins inside the roasting pan and pour hot water into the pan to reach two-thirds of the way up the sides of the ramekins. Bake until a small thin knife inserted in the center of one of the custards comes out clean, 45 to 60 minutes.

Carefully remove the pan from the oven. When the ramekins are cool enough to handle, lift them out of the water bath and let cool about 15 minutes. Cover with plastic wrap placed directly over the surface of the custard to prevent a skin from forming. Refrigerate until chilled, about 45 minutes and up to overnight.

To unmold, run a thin, sharp knife around the edge of the custard. Place a serving plate on top of each ramekin and invert together. Gently lift off the ramekin. Garnish each custard with a small dollop of whipped cream, if desired, and some of the strawberries.

Chapter 5

The Château Tells the Tale

A T least once in her young life, every girl has imagined herself as a princess in a fairy tale—we have Cinderella to thank for that. Brainwashed young, we donned glittering dresses at Halloween, danced waltzes in our living rooms in preparation for the royal ball, and, of course, dreamed of a castle of our very own. But what the bedtime tales of our youth neglected to tell us was just where to look for these enchanted landscapes and storybook abodes. Exactly where was Cinderella going in her horse-drawn carriage anyway? It could very well be she was headed here, to the Dordogne region of southwestern France, also known as the land of a thousand châteaux.

A local legend says that back when God was scattering castles over the kingdom of France, He got to the skies over the Dordogne and discovered that His bag had a hole in it, and tumbling out were crenellated towers and drawbridges. So, before returning to Paradise, God shook out the remaining "crumbs" from His sack over the rivers and valleys below. Traveling along the serpentine roads that span the Dordogne, we find this tale easy to believe. Every new curve seems to unveil a wondrous castle-crowned bluff.

I still recall the first time I saw the Château de Beynac looming over the Dordogne. I was driving to meet Chef Laura for the first time, assigned to write a magazine article about her culinary tour company. I rounded a curve and literally gasped out loud. I pulled over and called my husband. "You won't believe what I am

The imposing Château de Beynac that took my
breath away the first time I saw it.

looking at," was all I could think to say. I tried to describe it the best I could, but there are certain times when words don't suffice. This was one of them. Even though I have been visiting the region for years now, I still get goose bumps when I see Château de Beynac, and picture-perfect scenes still jump out to surprise me.

The Dordogne has inspired its fair share of fantasies and fairy tales, that's for sure, but it is more than just a playground for princesses. The many castles of the region bear witness to its tumultuous history, and evidence of the Hundred Years' War fought between England and France from 1337 to 1453 still scars many castle walls. These châteaux are also the birthplace of Périgord's gastronomic legacy. A tour of the large and well-equipped ancient kitchens, like the one at Château de Biron, and the *potagers* (kitchen gardens) shed light on the importance of cooking and cuisine during feudal times, when lords hired local farmers' daughters to prepare meals in their castles. These recipes have been refined and passed from generation to

generation and are the basis for today's traditional family recipes. We have spent a good deal of time visiting the brooding fortresses, like those of Bourdeilles, Beynac, Biron, and Castelnaud, but there are literally hundreds of smaller yet no less impressive castles and manor houses that have been lovingly restored and transformed into country estates, wineries, and private homes. A visit to any of them brings to light Dordogne's rich history, both recent and bygone.

Château des Milandes, for example, was built by François de Caumont, the proprietor of Château de Castelnaud, who had it erected in the fifteenth century for his young bride (she found the medieval fortress of Castelnaud a bit too unwelcoming). But the Château des Milandes is not remembered for its ancient history but rather its modern one. Over time, the château eventually fell into ruins but was famously restored in the 1930s by famous American music hall star Josephine Baker. It was there that she raised her twelve children and lived until she was forced to sell in 1968.

top: The inviting terrace at Château de Biron
bottom: Ancient kitchens tell the Dorgogne's culinary history.

Detour
PÉRIGORD DORDOGNE MONTGOLFIÈRES

A casual drive or kayak trip along one of the Dordogne's two main rivers is certain to provide great photo ops for château chasers, but arguably the best views come from above. Patrick Bécheau, a Saint-Cyprien native and owner and operator of hot air balloon company *Périgord Dordogne Montgolfières*, invited us "to step into his office," which happened to be a basket dangling like a charm from an enormous blue balloon. Not even the best penthouses in Manhattan could rival this, we thought, as we floated above some of the most stunning scenery imaginable. From a field near Beynac, we watched as flames shot into the blue mass of material, slowly giving the balloon its life. Once inflated, Patrick wasted no time in telling us to "jump in." Eight of us rose silently over the landscape, with only the blowing sound of more heat being fired into the balloon to break the silence. Over the fairy-tale châteaux and the sapphire river we drifted. We even spotted a few cafés, houses, and farms that were hidden behind the trees and would never have been visible from the road. At one point, several children ran below, yelling, "Bonjour." They followed us like the pied piper until we lifted over the trees and left them waving good-bye.

Morning and evening journeys are organized year-round, but the flights are dependent on good weather. We took an evening flight.

Patrick is a master at maneuvering, and he spun us around to point out distant horizons, including the castle of Biron, some sixty kilometers away, which he said was quite special to be able to see from such a distance. As usual, we had found another perfect night in the Dordogne.

Our adventure ended with a soft landing in a nameless pasture, where a picnic of walnuts, fruit, and locally distilled cider waited. Patrick solicited the guys to help deflate the balloon and somehow fold it and stuff it into a bag no bigger than a tent. Watching that was almost as fun as the ride itself. Almost. ■

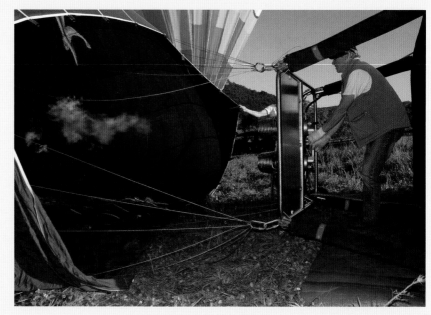

Over near Bergerac, a visit to the Château de Monbazillac, complete with moat, is interesting for any lover of architecture, with its combination of feudal defensive design and elegant Renaissance styling. The same can be said of Château de Lanquais, where the towers and parapets stand in contrast to the Renaissance interior furnishings and detail that give a picture of life during the Middle Ages. We especially love the old kitchen, where copper pots and lids that look like giant pizza cutters hang on the wall, and a fireplace large enough to roast an enemy army must have many stories to tell. On the property is also a restored tithe barn (renovated twenty years ago). A tithe barn was used in the Middle Ages for storing the *tithes*—a tenth of the farm's produce—which had to be given to the church. Today the barn is used for public concerts.

Though the large castles of the region are impressive and certainly make for great photographs and generate imaginative tales, it's the small chateaux that have been turned into private homes and bed-and-breakfasts, like the Château Lalinde, that have really stolen our hearts. Our home away from home for many years in the Dordogne was Le Prieuré au Château de Biron. Built for the priests, this former priory has been lovingly restored into a bed-and-breakfast, and is literally in the shadow of the castle of Biron. Rumor has it there is even a tunnel connecting the two, but we never found it. The majestic castle changed hands often between the English and French and was owned by fourteen generations of the Gontaut-Biron family until the State took it over in the twentieth century. A tour offers amazing views and a torture chamber (if you dare).

Around the Dordogne, the menacing iron gates and impenetrable walls of the châteaux remind us that these were places built to keep people out. Thankfully, things have changed. Where doors were once barriers to entry, they are now open and inviting. For lovers of history and architecture, the castles around the Dordogne are books that beckon us to read on. For those of you girls who dreamed of becoming princesses, welcome to Cinderella's happily ever after.

MY CHÂTEAU IS YOUR CHÂTEAU

"My being here is really serendipitous."

CROSSING THE DORDOGNE RIVER, where dozens of swans nimbly trace the ripples of water, we first spotted the timeless Château Lalinde, the sun casting a gold-dusted hue on its exterior wall and on shutters as ruby red as Snow White's apple. Well-tended flower boxes spilled over the railings, and windows and doors were opened wide to the fresh air of the Dordogne. We recognized immediately that a fairy tale was alive and well and living in Lalinde, the *bastide* (fortified medieval town) from which the castle draws its name.

Though she is not Snow White, Wilna Wilkinson is a modern-day princess living a luminous life in this riverfront retreat. "Sometimes I have to pinch myself," she admits in her lilting South African accent.

When she opens her door to us, the warmth of her heart and hearth is felt instantly. Wilna's walls and shelves are filled with paintings, books, and knickknacks that tell of her years of traveling the globe, but there is no question the Château Lalinde is her home, and she makes sure those who stay in one of her six guest rooms also feel as comfortable. We certainly did. Our room had books she thought we'd enjoy laid next to the bed, as well as a small box of chocolates "for a late-night sweet." The landing outside the rooms has cozy chairs and floor-to-ceiling bookshelves stuffed with travel guides, photos, and brochures to help us make the most of our stay.

Though it looks as if she has lived here all her life, it was only four years ago that fate intervened and altered her life's course. During a holiday with friends who had moved in nearby, Wilna suggested they enjoy a nice dinner out. They responded at once, "We know the perfect little place on the river that you will love." Their destination that evening was the Château Lalinde, and her friends were right—it *was* perfect, and Wilna *did* love it—so much so that two years to the date of the dinner, she moved into the château she now calls home: Kismet.

The living room where we sip an evening aperitif of Monbazillac wine was the former restaurant. It now houses two inviting sofas and a coffee table with fresh-cut flowers in the center. The tall French doors look out onto the river and an arched bridge. Wilna gazes out the window. "God, I love it here.

"My being here is really serendipitous." With that, she tells us her own modern fairy tale.

"I had casually said to my friends that night as we dined under the stars, 'I would move here tomorrow if it were for sale.' The waiter must have overheard me, because he said, 'But madame, the château *is* for sale.'" Even though she was not in the market for a castle (is anyone, really?), Wilna explains that she was looking for a change. She returned to her home in London, packed her belongings, and the rest is her very own happily ever after.

Out on the terrace, where a dining table is set beneath an iron candelabra, we have a view of the bridge lit up by the setting sun. It looks as though it's made of gold. The water from the river laps against the wall below, and Wilna

tells us that her sons like to fish from this spot. Wilna points to a small stone chapel above the river. "That's where the dragon died," she says matter-of-factly. With an intro like that, we had to know more. Legend has it that a dragon named Coulobre lived in the rocky druid caves opposite the village, terrorizing the locals. The dragon supposedly fell to its death from this site after a local bishop drove it away with the sign of the cross. Only the chapel and Wilna remain to perpetuate the story.

In the years that she has been in Lalinde, Wilna has learned French and immersed herself in a local's lifestyle, meeting her neighbors and exploring the region's villages, markets, and culture. We went to the market with her on Thursday morning, and she can hardly go ten steps without stopping to greet or kiss the cheeks of yet another friend. Remarkable is how they all light up when they see her, and even more remarkable is that she remembers each of their names and some small detail about them. "She is Dutch," she'll say, pointing to a cheese vendor. "He has a shop just over there," she says of a man selling gorgeous table linens. Her basket full of flowers and fresh produce (she insists on locally grown fruits and vegetables only), we make the five-minute walk back to her castle, and we realize that Wilna is as much a part of Lalinde as anyone here, and she is a true ambassador for the region.

She eagerly encourages visitors and transplanted foreigners alike to learn as much about the area as possible and is known to drag her guests to many of the regions must-see sites before bringing them home to enjoy a lovingly prepared meal. So dedicated is Wilna that she has turned her château into a residential learning center for newcomers to the Dordogne. She engages the help of locals to teach the language, give tours, and introduce expatriates to the customs, food, and history of the region. "If you want to know the people, you need to speak the language and understand their culture," she emphasizes.

The phone rings, and Wilna slips into her native Afrikaans, a language that to us is a beautiful blend of Dutch and Wilna charisma. Her exuberance for the region translates to her blog, where she serves up delightful advice and insight for any willing reader, from her views on local and national politics, to local festivals and markets, to some of her favorite local eateries, like Le P'tit Loup, and her favorite place for coffee, Hotel le Forêt.

We followed Wilna's advice and went to both. We met Bruno, the owner of Le P'tit Loup. Based on the vintage concert posters and the Carlos Santana music playing in the background, we're pretty sure he was a rock roadie in a former life. We also think that Le P'tit Loup serves one of the *best* omelettes we have ever tasted. Over at Hotel Le Forêt, owners Jean-Luc and Jean-Paul greet us like long-lost relatives. The coffee alone is worth the trip. Costa Rican,

Puerto Rican, Italian, French . . . you name it, they grind it and serve it with delicious *canéles* that are so perfectly crunchy on the outside, soft on the inside, we could eat ten more. We don't.

Wilna's repertoire of Dordogne details is comprehensive, but it's her love of food that has our stomachs growling. She rattles off names of her favorite Dordogne specialties, like the garlic soup at Restaurant de l'Abbaye in Cadouin. We later sampled it ourselves and agree the creamy concoction, served from a large tureen at your tableside, is something to try at least once. But Wilna really wins us over with a three-dimensional description of her latest culinary discovery, the *tourteau fromagé*, which she spotted at the Lalinde market. She describes them as "light-as-air fairy cakes neatly stacked in perfect little rows, like a class photograph of little schoolboys in their black caps." We eventually see the little cakes and smile. Wilna was right—they do look like schoolboys lined up for a class picture.

Wilna's in the kitchen now, preparing a farewell meal, and she stops to ask us to sign her guestbook. Like all things Wilna, there is nothing conventional about this either, and as we dip our hands in paint and leave the imprint on the wall in the kitchen and sign our names, we know we have touched her as much as she has touched us.

Wilna is living proof that it's not just the grand châteaux of the region that create happily ever after, but rather the gracious homes and the people who live within that make the Dordogne so utterly captivating to those of us fortuitous enough to be characters in the fairy tale. ∎

Wilna's "touching" guest book in her riverside castle

Périgourdine Garlic Soup

Also called *tourin blanchi*, this hearty peasant soup is traditionally brought to newlyweds in their bed on their wedding night. It is delicious and surprisingly simple to make, but there are many variations on the recipe. We recommend the *tourin blanchi* at the Restaurant de l'Abbaye in Cadouin. Or try our version here.

In a large stockpot over medium heat, melt the goose fat. Add the onions and garlic, and cook until the onions are tender but not brown, about 10 minutes. Stir in the flour until smooth. Add half of the stock and continue stirring until the mixture begins to thicken. Stir in the remaining stock and the beans (if using). Reduce the heat to medium-low and simmer for 45 minutes or until the beans are tender.

Working in batches, pour the soup into a blender and process until smooth. Return the soup to the stockpot and place over medium-low heat. Add the cream and season with salt and white pepper and the herbs. Adjust the heat until the soup is just simmering and slowly stir in the egg whites and vinegar.

Ladle the soup into a tureen or bowls, float large pieces of the bread on top, if using, and serve right away. If you are bringing the soup to newlyweds, don't forget to knock!

MAKES 6 SERVINGS

3 tablespoons (43 g) goose fat or shortening

2 large yellow onions, chopped

8 garlic cloves, minced

¼ cup (30 g) all-purpose flour

8 cups (2 liters) chicken or duck stock

½ cup (115 g) dried white beans, soaked overnight (optional)

1 cup (250 ml) heavy whipping cream or crème fraîche

Coarse salt and white pepper

Chopped fresh herbs (parsley, chives, thyme)

2 egg whites, beaten

1 tablespoon (15 ml) white vinegar

1 day-old baguette, sliced 2 inches (5 cm) thick (optional)

Roast Chicken with Chanterelles, Fingerling Potatoes, and Garlic Cream Sauce

MAKES 4 SERVINGS

1 large chicken (about 4 lb/2 kg)

¼ pound (125 g) unsalted butter, melted

Coarse salt and cracked pepper

12 small, red vine-ripened tomatoes (about ½ pound/250 g total)

1 pound (500 g) chanterelle mushrooms, brushed clean and stemmed

8 shallots, unpeeled

¾ pound (375 g) fingerling or small new potatoes

4 cups (1 liter) heavy whipping cream

4 garlic cloves, peeled

½ cup (30 g) loosely packed fresh basil leaves

Once upon a time, cooking with cream was considered a luxury reserved for the wealthy. This simple chicken is dressed with a regal cream sauce, transforming it into an elegant dish fit for a king.

———————————— ● ● ————————————

Preheat the oven to 400°F (200°C).

Rinse the chicken and pat dry with paper towels. Place the chicken in a roasting pan, brush with some of the melted butter, and season with salt and pepper. Roast until the juices run clear and a meat thermometer inserted into the thickest part of the thigh reads 175°F (79°C), about 1 hour. Let rest for 10 minutes before carving. Maintain the oven temperature.

Using 4 small baking pans for the vegetables, place the tomatoes, mushrooms, shallots, and potatoes each in their own pan. Brush the vegetables with some of the melted butter and season with salt and pepper. Roast the vegetables until tender, about 10 minutes for the tomatoes, 15 minutes for the mushrooms, and about 20 minutes for the shallots and the potatoes. Cover the potatoes with aluminum foil to keep warm until assembly.

While the vegetables are roasting, prepare the sauce. In a medium saucepan over medium heat, warm the cream and garlic to just below a boil. Reduce the heat to low and simmer, stirring occasionally, until reduced by half, about 20 minutes.

Pour the garlic cream sauce into a blender or food processor. Purée until smooth. Return half of the sauce to the saucepan and place over low heat to keep warm. Add the basil leaves to the remaining sauce in the blender and purée until smooth and green. Pour into another small saucepan and place over low heat to keep warm.

To carve the chicken, using a small, sharp pairing knife, carefully cut the breast meat from the chicken, starting at the top of the breastbone. Loosen the meat from the bones and cut down to the thigh. Insert the knife into the thigh joint to remove the thigh, and then cut the leg from the thigh. Keep the skin intact for serving. Slice each breast in half crosswise.

For each serving, place a chicken thigh or leg in a large, shallow dinner bowl and stack half of a breast on top. Arrange the roasted potatoes and mushrooms around the chicken. Ladle each of the two sauces over half of the dish, keeping the sauces separate. Garnish with the roasted tomatoes and shallots.

Grilled Prime Rib of Beef with Garlic and Rosemary

Imagine the aroma and sizzle from the château hearth as this impressive piece of meat roasts over an open fire. A gas or charcoal grill, our modern-day equivalent, makes a perfect, crusty-on-the-outside, tender-on-the-inside prime rib. Ask your butcher to trim the bones to about 3 inches (7.5 cm) and the fat cap to 1 to 2 inches (2.5 to 5 cm).

◆ ◈ ◆

Set up a gas or charcoal grill for indirect cooking. If using a gas grill, preheat to medium-low heat.

Using a small, thin knife, pierce the surface of the meat at 2-inch (5-cm) intervals. Insert the garlic slivers and fresh rosemary sprigs into the openings. In a small bowl, combine the salt, pepper, dried rosemary, and flour. Rub the mixture all over the meat to coat.

Place the roast, fat side up, on the hot grate directly over the drip pan. Cover and grill the meat. If using a charcoal grill, add 10 to 12 fresh coals on each side every hour. If the grill seems too hot, reduce the heat or move charcoal further to the side of the grill away from the meat. If using a gas grill, keep the lid closed at all times.

Using an instant-read thermometer, check the temperature after about 3 hours of grilling. Continue grilling until the meat is cooked to your desired degree of doneness, 145°F (63°C) or 3½ to 4 hours for medium-rare. The meat will continue to cook after it is removed from the heat.

Transfer the roast to a platter or carving board and cover loosely with aluminum foil.

Let rest at least 10 to 15 minutes before carving and serving.

MAKES 12 SERVINGS

1 prime rib beef roast
(16 to 18 lb/7 to 8 kg total)

6 garlic cloves, quartered lengthwise

6 sprigs fresh rosemary, cut into
2-inch pieces

2 tablespoons coarse salt

2 tablespoons cracked pepper

2 tablespoons dried rosemary

2 tablespoons (12.5 g)
all-purpose flour

Walnut-Crowned Noisette of Lamb with Black Currant Jus

The tartness of the black currants is a delightful contrast to the sweetness of the walnuts and lamb. After browning in a frying pan, the lamb is finished in the oven to create a delicate "crown" of walnuts. The perfect dish for your royal family gatherings.

Trim the excess fat from the lamb loins and season well with salt and pepper. Rub the loins with the mustard and roll it in the walnuts. Cover and refrigerate until ready to use.

In a large, heavy frying pan over medium-high heat, melt 1 tablespoon of the goose fat. Place 1 or 2 of the lamb loins in the pan, being careful not to overcrowd the pan, and cook until browned, about 4 minutes. With as little handling as possible, carefully turn the loins and continue cooking until the other side is browned, about 4 minutes. Reduce the heat slightly, if necessary. Transfer the loins to a roasting pan. Add the remaining goose fat to the pan, if needed, and cook the remaining loins. The loins may be prepared up to 4 hours ahead and refrigerated until ready to roast.

Preheat the oven to 400°F (200°C).

Roast the loins, uncovered, for about 10 minutes for rare and 12 to 14 minutes for medium rare. Let rest for 10 minutes before slicing.

To make the black currant *jus*, melt the butter in a large saucepan over medium-high heat. Add the currants and cook for about 1 minute. Add the wine and cook until it reduces by half, about 12 minutes. Add the stock and continue cooking until the sauce lightly coats the back of a spoon, about 10 minutes. Season with salt and pepper. If desired, pour the *jus* through a fine-mesh sieve to strain out the currants. Depending on the tartness of the currants, you may want to sweeten the *jus* with 1 teaspoon honey. Keep the *jus* warm until ready to serve.

Using a sharp knife, cut the loins into approximately 1½-inch (4-cm) medallions (*noisettes*). Arrange 3 medallions, cut side up, on each serving plate. Drizzle the *jus* over the medallions and serve right away.

MAKES 6 SERVINGS

2 pounds (1 kg) boneless lamb loin, cut crosswise into 4 pieces

Coarse salt and cracked pepper

2 tablespoons walnut or Dijon mustard

1½ cups (185 g) finely chopped walnuts

2 tablespoons (29 g) goose fat or butter, divided

For the black currant *jus*:

1 tablespoon (14 g) unsalted butter

1 cup (125 g) fresh black currants

2 cups (500 ml) Pécharmant or dry Bordeaux wine

1 cup (250 ml) beef or veal stock

Coarse salt and cracked pepper

Honey as needed

Tourteau Fromagé

These delightful goat cheese cakes are originally from the Poitou-Charentes region along the Atlantic coast. Thanks to Wilna, we spotted them at the Lalinde market. We agree with her that the "black caps" probably first appeared by accident, but they have become part of their idiosyncratic appearance. There is a special mold for these cakes, but a pie dish works just as well.

———————————————————●●————————————————————

To make the pastry, place the flour in a large bowl and scatter the butter over the top. Using a fork, toss the butter to coat with the flour. Using a pastry blender or two knives, cut in the butter until the mixture forms large, coarse crumbs the size of large peas.

Whisk together the egg yolks and ¼ cup (60 ml) of the water. Add to the butter-flour mixture and, using a spoon, stir until a soft ball forms. Add more water, if needed. Wrap the dough in plastic wrap and refrigerate until well chilled, about 1 hour.

On a lightly floured work surface, roll the dough out into a round 10 inches (25 cm) in diameter and ½ inch (12 mm) thick. Press the dough into an 8-inch (20-cm) pie dish and trim the edges, if necessary. Cover and chill until ready to use.

Preheat the oven to 375°F (190°C).

To make the filling, in a large mixing bowl, beat the egg whites and half of the sugar with a balloon whisk until stiff.

In another large mixing bowl, beat the butter, goat cheese, milk, salt, and the remaining sugar until well blended. Beat in the egg yolks one at a time until incorporated. Add the flour and vanilla and mix until incorporated. Gently fold half of the beaten egg whites into the mixture until incorporated. Fold in the remaining egg whites. Pour the batter into the pastry crust.

Bake until the center is firm or a toothpick inserted into the center of the cake comes out clean, about 45 minutes. Remove from the oven. Using a kitchen torch, quickly and evenly blacken the top of the cake. Alternatively, raise the oven temperature to 550°F (290°C), place the pie dish under the broiler, and broil until the top of the cake blackens. Let cool.

Slice and serve at room temperature.

MAKES ONE 8-INCH (20-CM) CAKE

For the pastry:

1 ½ cups (185 g) all-purpose flour

¼ pound (125 g) cold butter, cut into ¾-inch (2-cm) pieces

2 large egg yolks

¼ cup (60 ml) cold water, plus more as needed

For the filling:

6 large eggs, separated

¾ cup (185 g) sugar, divided

4 tablespoons (60 g) unsalted butter, melted

½ pound (250 g) fresh goat cheese

1 tablespoon (15 ml) milk

⅛ teaspoon salt

3 tablespoons all-purpose flour

1 teaspoon (15 ml) vanilla extract

Chapter 6

Fair and Square

TOURING around France's small back roads is admittedly a thrill, but let's be honest—after a few hundred "quaint villages," they all start to look the same. When we first arrived in the Dordogne, we noticed a square checkerboard symbol below certain village names and experienced revived excitement at discovering something new. These icons, we learned, indicated that we were entering a *bastide*, or medieval "new town." While these villages are also quaint, they are different from your typical European village, yet similar to one another, and it's this conformity that makes them one of the region's most unique and historic hallmarks.

The *bastides* of the Dordogne are living monuments to a time of great strife in the region, as well as a glimpse at early urban planning. During the Hundred Years' War between France and England, kings founded the *bastides* in order to keep their populations loyal and to broaden their control. They were also economic centers that attracted people to the towns with parcels of land on which to build houses as well as farming plots outside the town gates. These town residents were then obliged to organize armies and defend their benefactors in wars and pay taxes on their residences and trade. In the Dordogne approximately twenty-five *bastides* were begun during the Middle Ages, but only eighteen were completed.

The empty and tiny bastide of Molièrs

If you look at most European villages, the church occupies the most prominent position, while in *bastides* the market square is the focal point and is a defining characteristic of the *bastides*—an indicator of the importance of commerce and trade during the time they were built. Another feature shared by the *bastides* is their careful positions within their surroundings. Some were built on hilltops with high vantage points for protection, like the lofty locales of Monflanquin, Castillonnès, and Domme, while towns like Eymet and Lalinde, the first English-built *bastide*, were set up at strategic points along rivers.

Bastides all had outer walls and secured gates to protect inhabitants from intruders, but these gates also controlled entry into and exit from the profitable market square. Many of the *bastides* still show off the remnants of their ancient fortifications, some more impressive than others, like the Porte des Tours in Domme, named for the two round guard towers that flank the entrance. In 1307, these towers were converted into prisons where the Knights Templar were confined after being arrested by the king. Rivalry among the *bastides* was fierce.

On the terrace at one of our favorite cafés, Bistrot 2, just outside one of Monpazier's primitive gates, we heard an interesting anecdote. We were told that one night the rulers of Monpazier decided to raid Villefranche-du-Périgord. Coincidentally, on the very same night, Villefranche-du-Périgord's leaders decided to invade Monpazier. By chance each took a different route, and each was pleased to find their target undefended and easy to take. They returned to their respective villages with their loot, only to find their own homes ransacked. The two *bastides* struck an agreement, and both sides returned their spoils. Who knows

if this is true, but sipping wine on the cobblestones of Monpazier, we could almost hear the approaching horse hooves!

Within the walls and gates of the *bastides* are displayed their most distinctive feature: a grid layout with streets intersecting at ninety-degree angles around the main square. Anyone who has navigated an old European city knows that "going around the block" is rarely possible. For a real sense of what a typical French town layout looks like . . . drop a handful of cooked spaghetti on the ground, *et voilà*! Indeed, Europe's villages and cities are notorious for their twisting and disobedient roads, the bane of lost tourists (and writers) everywhere. While we'd like to believe the grid plan of the *bastides* was created to help disoriented visitors, it was actually conceived for the ease of finding residents and collecting their taxes.

Monpazier is considered the "perfect" *bastide*, a masterpiece for its pristine condition and grid system. Little has changed there since King Edward I of England founded it in 1285. The covered area of the market, the *halle,* and its grain measures used to calculate taxes is still visible in here, as well as in Villefranche-du-Périgord, and even today, the marketplaces in the *bastides* remain the nucleus of social and commercial activity. A walk around Monpazier gives a real sense of just how these new towns were constructed according to well-defined rules and standards. Arches and covered walkways are prevalent around market squares; the width of the streets, alleys, and other passageways in the *bastides* was all predetermined, as was the tiny space between houses, which was calculated to the millimeter. Called an *androne*, this small gap was designed to prevent fires from spreading and to allow for drainage—enlightened thinking for the Dark Ages!

One of the strangest experiences we had was our accidental visit (we got lost following a sign to a walnut farm) to the unfinished *bastide* of Molières. The town was founded in 1284 but ravaged by the Hundred Years' War, rebuilt, only to be destroyed again during the Wars of Religion. It is graced with a Gothic church, only one arcade, a market square (no *halle* was ever built), remnants of a fortress, and has only 300 inhabitants—301, if you count the ghost. Rumor has it that the aptly named Pedro the Cruel poisoned his wife, Blanca of Castile, here in the 1360s. Allegedly, her ghost still strolls the streets of Molières today. On the day

Detour
CADOUIN ABBEY

IN a narrow valley south of the Dordogne River is the town of Cadouin (full name Le-Buisson-de-Cadouin), not far from Molières. One of our favorite restaurants, Restaurant de L'Abbeye, is here and serves our favorite tourin blanchi (garlic soup) in the region. As much as we'd like to think we discovered Cadouin ourselves, this easy-to-miss-if-you-blink town was discovered long before we arrived, thanks to an abbey of the same name, built in 1115, and a piece of embroidered linen believed to be the shroud that enveloped the head of Jesus in the tomb. Cadouin became Périgord's most prestigious abbey, and for eight centuries it prospered greatly from the pilgrimages, among the most famous visitors being Richard the Lionheart and Eleanor of Aquitaine. During the Hundred Years' War, the cloister was destroyed and the cloth was moved to Toulouse for protection. It was returned to Cadouin in 1453. In the 1930s the cloth was found to date from the eleventh century and thus deemed not at all authentic. The pilgrimages stopped immediately, but the beautiful cloth is still on display here. Cadouin Abbey is now a UNESCO World Heritage Site and a part of the pilgrimage route to Santiago de Compostela in Spain.

Today, the Abbey still draws visitors to its beautiful Gothic cloisters, built in the fifteenth and sixteenth centuries. For us, the idea that so many men and women of history stood on this very site was awesome. On the day we visited, there were clouds and rain, and the cloisters were dark. We were alone, and we walked the square silently, observing the carvings and iconography, and of course, the cloth that launched a thousand pilgrimages. We were about to leave, literally with a hand on the door to exit, when something inspired us to turn around. As we did, the sun beamed through the cloisters and cast an ethereal reflection on the ground. It lasted only ten seconds, but we caught the image with our camera. The shadows faded into the gray cement again, and we had to wonder how many others over the last eight centuries witnessed this same heavenly light. ∎

we arrived, it would have been nice to see someone, anyone (even poor Blanca). The streets were eerily empty and silent, and we didn't see a single person on the street; there was not a shop open; not a sound. We got out of the car when we saw a sign for *Maison de Noix* (house of walnuts). It wasn't a farm, but it would have to do. It, too, was closed. We wandered down the straight streets, under the one arcade, and onto the cream-colored gravel that covers the market square. Even though there was no one around, we felt we had to whisper to one another—it was that quiet. Nearby, we noticed a lone crate of walnuts. It started to drizzle, and we wondered to whom this crate belonged. Out of nowhere, a man in a purple sweater and beret (yes, really, a beret) shuffled toward us. We tried to ask him where everyone was, whether or not the walnut house would open, and if we could take his photo. He said nothing, picked up his crate, and kept moving, only offering this: "My nuts are getting wet." We snapped a photo anyway, and it remains one of our favorites. It's out of focus (from laughing too hard, maybe), but the memory of Molières and our "walnut guy" is clear.

We went back to Molières on another day, in a different year, to see if, by chance, we just missed something. It was exactly the same. Still eerily quiet and empty, and like all the *bastides*, still a unique part of Dordogne history.

Grain measures were used to calculate cost in many of the bastide halles.

Our favorite walnut guy

Porte des Tours, Domme

IN THE MOOD FOR FOOD

HENRY MILLER WROTE, "Just to glimpse the black, mysterious river at Domme from the beautiful bluff is something to be grateful for all one's life." Sitting on the terrace with our feet propped up on the railing, it is easy to understand what he meant.

We've made ourselves quite at home here in Domme and the Hotel-Restaurant L'Esplanade. During our first trip to the Dordogne, we vowed this would be our "secret place." L'Esplanade proved too good to keep to ourselves, and we have been bringing friends and guests here ever since. The restaurant has some of the best and most creative food in the region, but what has made L'Esplanade so special to us is the family that runs it and the zany chef in the kitchen.

When we arrive today, chef Pascal Bouland is stressed out. He is rubbing his hands through his hair and pacing, mumbling unintelligible French words pierced with the occasional "*Oh-là-là!*" we have grown to appreciate. He says sarcastically, holding his thumb an inch from his index finger, "I have a little problem." Pascal's oven is broken, and he is waiting for delivery of a new one so he and his team can prepare dinner for the fully reserved dining room tonight. Still, Pascal and his wife, Sophie, greet us with a kiss on both cheeks and smile, the same way they have for years. Sophie's mother, Monique, is behind the bar and prepares us coffee and pastries before we sit down at a table in the salon of their hotel/home that looks a bit like a saloon on an old movie set. Despite his understandable anxiety,

Pascal's sharp wit, quirky facial expressions, and perfectly groomed mustache put us at ease and make us laugh until our cheeks hurt. Even the image on the menu at L'Esplanade, a picture of four geese roasting a chef, reveals his sense of humor. Pascal claims he feels like that chef on many days, and it's no surprise his food is often an extension of his mood. "I never create when I am angry," he jokes. "Otherwise the clients might not pay the bill."

Kidding aside, Pascal is a serious chef who takes pride in expressing emotion with his food. He believes a meal infused with several different tastes will prolong the experience for the diner, allowing him to savor each flavor. He explains, "I often ask myself, 'What do I feel like today? What would I like to taste? And how can I do it?'"

His energy is then set in full artistic motion. He says it's not uncommon for him to wake up in the middle of the night and jot down an idea for a menu or a dish in his notebook. Judging by the hulking binder on his lap, he hasn't been sleeping much. "When an idea hits me at night when I am in bed, I have to get up and write it down," says Pascal. He likens the book to an artist's sketchpad, and inside are pages and pages of diagrams, ingredients, recipes, menus, photos, and miniscule details, like how the food is to be plated. We lean in to get a closer look, even take a picture, but Pascal closes the notebook gently and, grinning, wags his finger side to side. "An artist has his secrets," he teases.

Like his moods, Pascal's creations cover a broad spectrum, and while typical dishes of the Périgord are available,

his menu is not limited to the classics. Born and raised in this culinary region, he is intimate with the bounty available to him. He starts with local ingredients as a base for his dishes, but then fuses them with something out of the ordinary, "I love to create new flavors. For example, I love seafood, like lobster, which is not from the Périgord. But then I pair it with the black truffles, and, voilà! It is the old with the new." Pascal makes more than 150 different recipes but has double the ideas. For his regular clients, he often creates something off the menu. "We still have our traditional dishes, but our clients today don't eat like our clients of twenty years ago. So, we must adapt and more importantly, surprise."

L'Esplanade has been in the family for over two decades, and prior to Pascal, it was Sophie's father, René, who ran the kitchen. We ask Pascal if he learned a lot from his father and he is quick to correct us with a smile, "Father-in-law, not father," then deadpans, "It's not the same."

Pascal is in quite a mood. We can only imagine what's in store for diners tonight! He laughs nervously, suddenly remembering the calamity unfolding in his kitchen. "Tonight, they are in for a real treat," he says, raising his eyebrows up and down.

Back on the terrace, with our feet up, we watch the day sink into night, and remember why we keep coming back to L'Esplanade—it puts us in a good mood to see Domme the way Henry Miller did. Peering through the window at the satisfied faces around the dining room, we can see that tonight, Pascal's mood is also good. ■

Symmetry in Dordogne's bastides

Cèpes Farcis
(Stuffed Porcini Mushrooms)

According to our favorite ice cream man, Roland Manouvrier (see chapter 4), these stuffed *cèpes* (porcini mushrooms) are rarely found on menus anymore, and as he recounted his grandmother's traditional dish, we knew we had to try it ourselves. Like so many *Périgourdine* recipes, hers was never written down, just passed on from table to table. Gather the mushrooms from the world-famous *cèpes* market in the *bastides* of Monpazier or Villefranche-du-Périgord, and enjoy them as a side dish or on their own.

Preheat the oven to 350°F (180°C).

Remove the stems from the mushrooms and arrange the caps in a large baking dish. Finely chop the stems and place them in a bowl.

Scrape off the excess fat from each leg of duck confit; remove and discard the skin and bones. Using your fingers, tear the meat into small pieces. Add the duck meat to the bowl with the mushrooms stems. Add the garlic and parsley and mix well to combine. Season with salt and pepper. Add the bread pieces and mix until the stuffing sticks together.

Spoon the stuffing into the mushroom caps, dividing it evenly among them. Drizzle the wine over the mushrooms and scatter the tomatoes on top.

Bake, uncovered, until the mushrooms pierce easily with a fork, about 60 minutes. Serve right away.

MAKES 4 SERVINGS

8 large porcini mushrooms, about 3 inches (7.5 cm) in diameter, brushed clean

3 legs Duck Confit (see page 46)

1 garlic clove, minced

¼ cup (15 g) chopped fresh parsley

Coarse salt and cracked pepper

5 oz (150 g) baguette with crust removed, torn into small pieces

1 cup (250 ml) dry white wine

4 medium tomatoes, diced

Pumpkin Bisque
with Cèpes and Potato Straws

The woodsy flavor of the *cèpes* (porcini mushrooms) and the crunchiness of the potato straws add a slightly different twist to this silky fall favorite. You can prepare the potato straws up to one day ahead of time and store in an airtight container.

In a small bowl, soak the porcini mushrooms in the warm water until softened, about 15 minutes. Strain the mushrooms, reserving the liquid. Cut the mushrooms into thin strips.

In a large stockpot over medium heat, melt the butter. Add the onion and cook until it begins to soften, about 10 minutes. Stir in the flour and cook for 1 minute. Add 3 cups (750 ml) of the stock and continue stirring until the liquid is smooth and just starting to thicken, 12 to 15 minutes. Add the remaining stock, the reserved mushroom liquid, the pumpkin cubes, 1 tablespoon salt, and the cayenne pepper. Simmer over low heat until the pumpkin is soft, about 30 minutes.

Pour into a blender or food processor and purée until smooth. Return the purée to the pot and add the mushrooms, nutmeg, saffron, and sherry. Simmer over low heat, stirring occasionally, until heated through and small bubbles appear around the edges, about 20 minutes.

Meanwhile, cut the potatoes into ⅛-inch-thick (3-mm) slices using a mandoline. Stack the slices and cut them lengthwise into thin strips. In a medium saucepan over medium-high heat, warm the oil until it sizzles when a few of the potato strips are added. Fry the strips until crisp and golden brown, about 3 minutes. Using a wire-mesh skimmer, transfer the strips to paper towels to drain. Season lightly with salt.

Just before serving, stir the crème fraîche and parsley into the soup. Taste and adjust the seasonings. Ladle the soup into bowls and garnish with crumbled bacon and a small handful of the potato straws.

MAKES 6 SERVINGS

5 oz (155 g) dried porcini mushrooms

½ cup (125 ml) warm water
(120°F/49°C)

4 tablespoons (60 g) unsalted butter

1 large yellow onion, chopped

⅓ cup (40 g) all-purpose flour

6 cups (1.5 liters) chicken stock, divided

1 pound (500 g) pumpkin,
peeled and cubed

Coarse salt

1 teaspoon cayenne pepper

½ teaspoon ground nutmeg

Pinch of saffron threads

¼ cup (60 ml) dry sherry

2 large russet or white potatoes, peeled

2 cups (500 ml) vegetable oil

1 cup (8 fl oz/250 ml) crème fraîche

¼ cup (15 g) chopped fresh parsley

6 strips bacon, cooked and
crumbled, for garnish

L'Enchaud Périgourdine

We enjoyed this traditional Dordogne–style pot roast at Le Bistro d'en Face in Trémolat. We tried to get the recipe, but they would not part with it, so we created our own version. Using the method for preserving duck, the chef laces pork loin with garlic and slowly cooks the meat in goose fat until tender. Our version is served cold with a warm potato salad for a savory summer lunch.

———————————●●———————————

MAKES 6 SERVINGS

3 garlic cloves, minced

1 teaspoon chopped fresh thyme

2 teaspoons coarse salt, divided

2 tablespoons cracked pepper, divided

1 pork loin roast (about 3 lb/1.5 kg), butterflied

4 tablespoons (60 g) goose fat or shortening

2 cups (500 ml) chicken stock

In a small bowl, combine the garlic, thyme, 1 teaspoon of the salt, and 1 tablespoon of the pepper.

Unroll the pork roast, flatten it, and trim any excess fat. Rub the loin with the garlic-thyme mixture. Roll the loin into a cylinder and tie at 3-inch (7.5-cm) intervals with kitchen string. Season with the remaining salt and pepper and refrigerate overnight.

Preheat the oven to 350°F (180°C).

In a Dutch oven over medium heat, melt the goose fat. Add the loin and brown well on all sides. Add the stock and cover. Transfer to the oven and roast, basting occasionally, until a thermometer registers 150°F (66°C), 1½ to 2 hours.

Transfer the loin to a deep dish and let cool. With a spoon, skim the fat from the cooking liquid. Pour the liquid over the loin and chill in the refrigerator overnight.

Untie the loin and cut it into thick slices. Serve cold with the meat jelly (the gelled cooking liquid) from the dish and Warm Potato Salad with Walnut-Mustard Vinaigrette (next page).

Warm Potato Salad
with Walnut-Mustard Vinaigrette

This warm potato salad is a nice complement to the cold *L'Enchaud Périgour-dine* (previous page) or as part of a fall picnic. The vinaigrette is poured on while the potatoes are still warm to infuse the flavors.

———◆◗◆◖◆———

Fill a large pot with salted water and bring to a boil over high heat. Cook the potatoes until just tender, 12 to 15 minutes.

Meanwhile, in a small bowl, combine the mustard, garlic, and vinegar. Whisk in the walnut oil a few drops at a time until the vinaigrette begins to emulsify. Add the olive oil and continue stirring. Add the salt and pepper.

Drain the potatoes, place in a large bowl, and let cool slightly. Pour the vinaigrette over the potatoes and toss to coat well. Add the chives and parsley. Taste, adjust seasonings, and serve warm.

MAKES 6 SERVINGS

2 pounds (1 kg) small new
potatoes, halved

2 tablespoons Dijon mustard

1 garlic clove, minced

¼ cup (60 ml) walnut vinegar

¼ cup (60 ml) walnut oil

¼ cup (60 ml) olive oil

1 teaspoon coarse salt

2 teaspoons cracked pepper

½ cup (30 g) minced fresh chives

½ cup (30 g) chopped fresh parsley

Pascal's Strawberries with Monbazillac Sabayon

MAKES 6 SERVINGS

10 extra-large egg yolks

1 cup (250 ml) Monbazillac, Sauternes
or other sweet dessert wine

1 cup (250 g) sugar

3 pints (750 g) *mara des bois* or
other strawberries

The sweet wine of Monbazillac is made from grapes allowed to ripen on the vines until the famous noble rot has worked its magic. This delightful recipe, shared by Pascal Bouland at L'Esplanade in Domme, combines the wine with exquisite local strawberries, like the *mara des bois*, found in local markets.

❖

In a large bowl, combine the egg yolks, wine, and sugar and mix well.

Set the bowl over a saucepan filled halfway with barely simmering water (the bowl should not touch the water). With a wire whisk, beat vigorously until the egg mixture is light and frothy and begins to thicken. Reduce the heat to low and continue whisking until the mixture reaches the consistency of lightly whipped cream. Remove from the heat and immediately pour into a clean bowl. Let cool, stirring every few minutes to prevent a film from forming on top.

Slice the strawberries in half, if desired. Divide the strawberries evenly among 6 coupe glasses and spoon the sabayon over the top.

Chapter 7

Fêtes Fit for a King

ONE of the many things we love about the Dordogne is its willingness to whoop it up, be it at a public street festival or a private celebration. During the summer not a weekend goes by without a *fête* (celebration), but the Dordogne is really a year-round party. Whether honoring the season, the wine, or an ancient way of life, these convivial scenes bring out droves of locals eager to share their music and customs. A copy of *Fêtes en Périgord*, a free booklet with up-to-date details of festivals and cultural events throughout the region, is available at any tourist office and is a good place to find a party. The calendar is jam-packed with something to suit any taste. Flip through and you will see that there is always a reason to celebrate Dordogne-style.

On June 24 La Fête de St. Jean heralds the arrival of summer and one of the sweetest traditions of the Périgord. The residents make crosses out of wild flowers that are then placed above entry doors to houses or barns (to protect the livestock). Recently, our friend Roland was a bit miffed at his fellow St. Léon neighbors who had, in his opinion, not taken the proper care to honor the tradition. "Many of them just made them from their garden flowers," he complained. I asked him if it really mattered if the crosses were made from wild flowers and wasn't the sentiment the same? "Maybe people don't have time these days to search for wildflowers?" I offered. "NO!" he insisted. "You must frolic in the hills

Village fetes, like this one in Biron, are a part of summertime in the Dordogne.

and appreciate the liberty and freedom of finding the wild flowers; then make the cross." That's life in a fairy tale, I guess.

In July and August, many villages hold their annual *bodegas*, that is, street parties organized by the local rugby club as a fund-raiser. Bands play into the wee hours, and food and wine are plentiful. Among our favorites are the bodegas of Issigeac, Villereal, and Castillonnes. Eymet launched its own in 2005, and a healthy rivalry between the towns means the parties keep getting bigger and better. Medieval festivals in the *bastides*, especially in Monpazier, are spectacles with over-the-top garb and merriment for all ages. On the third weekend in July, basket makers from all over the region descend on Issigeac to demonstrate their craft at the *Foire aux Panniers* (basket fair). A book festival called *Estivalivre* is held every first Wednesday in August in Buisson-de-Cadouin, and the amazing *Félibrée* takes place on July 1 in a different village each year. This traditional festival honors the Occitan heritage and language (*Langue d'oc*), but it also summons the most spectacular display of paper flowers we have ever seen. These are not crepe paper decorations for the gymnasium dance, but rather thousands and thousands of handmade blossoms in a variety of colors suspended over the cobbled streets and squares. The *Félibrée* begins with morning mass (in Occitan), followed by a banquet called the *Taulade*. The rest of the day is surrendered to the traditional music, dance, theater, and poetry of the troubadours while onlookers, often dressed in costume too, dance in the streets. Périgueux in early August means the International Contemporary Mime Festival with street artists, theater performances, and even workshops for dedicated mime enthusiasts (or for the travel buddies you want to keep quiet for a while).

This is the Dordogne, so naturally food is a favorite theme of some savory celebrations. The festival *Les Tables de Cyrano* invites Bergerac's restaurants, shops, and purveyors to set up in the streets for three days of tasting amid special events, music, and fireworks. The name of the festival recalls Cyrano de Bergerac, the French playwright with whom the town shares its name and to whom it owes some of its fame. Though the dramatist has no connection to the village, never having lived or traveled there, a statue commemorating him amuses tourists nonetheless.

Rocamadour is not only a spectacular village hewn into the side of a cliff and a stop on the pilgrimage to Santiago de Compostela, but it is also the divine site of the largest annual cheese festival in southern France. Usually in late May or early June, the event is replete with gooey and stinky curds. For those who like to take it slow, literally, there is the annual snail festival in the small village of Bertric-Burée near

THERE are not many places in the world where tradition marries so seamlessly with gastronomic excellence, but here in the Dordogne (and around France, for that matter) a network of *fermes auberges* (farmhouse inns) have opened their doors and serve up typical regional cuisine in unique countryside settings with products grown on their own properties. There are roughly two hundred farms around the Dordogne, and menus range from three courses to seven, costing anywhere from thirteen to thirty euros, wine included. The best part: the owners are right there in the kitchen and dining room. Like going home for dinner, a trip to a farmhouse inn is worthy of your time and is a way of life here.

There are many to choose from in the region. We like the charming Ferme Auberge D'Imbes in Archignac, where traditional foie gras and confit de canard by owners Cathy and Serge are served on the outside terrace surrounded by open fields. Les Truffières in Trémolat has also earned a reputation as one of the best. But our favorite auberge outing is to the Ferme Auberge Maraval in Cénac et Saint Julien, not far from Domme. We scooted past the ducks wandering near the cars and into the dining room, where a party of thirty was already in full swing. We squeezed into a table, and Eric immediately poured us some homemade walnut wine. For the next three hours, Sandrine cooked divine Dordogne cuisine and Eric expertly managed the large table of French tourists from Lyon, our table and two others, and a dogfight in the garden. Professional waiters in top hotels couldn't do it better. The stream of plates was endless. We had soup, foie gras, *magret, pommes sardalaises*, white asparagus, salad, walnut cake, coffee, and more wine. Where we put it is still a mystery.

When things calmed down a bit, Eric sat at a table near ours and began talking to people who had clearly been there before. He was explaining the sound a Harley-Davidson motorcycle makes, calling it distinct, then added for my benefit, "much like the American accent." He winked. He knew I was eavesdropping (how else am I going to learn new vocabulary words?). We all laughed, and like that, we were part of the group, invited for more wine, and we chatted for another thirty minutes. When Eric got up to say good-bye to a guest, the lady at the table, perhaps thinking I was offended by Eric's comment, patted my arm and said, "Don't worry; your accent is part of your charm." I wasn't offended at all. On the contrary, I felt more comfortable than ever. After all, where else but among close friends and family can you laugh with (and at) one another?

Along with excellent regional cuisine, you can count on familiarity and comfort at the *fermes auberges* in the Dordogne—it's the reason we go back again and again. ∎

Our dear friend, Sally Evans

Ribérac on the first Monday in May. No snail races (that could take a while), just good eating. Naturally, around Bergerac, wine celebrations runneth over during the fall harvest.

We have fêted into the wee hours in some of the most picturesque villages imaginable. But the cherry on top of our Périgord party sundae is the annual village fête in the hamlet of Biron. Our first visit sold us, and for years after, it seemed we were as much a part of the Biron party scene as the fireworks and polka music.

To be sure, it is not the pageantry that lures us back year after year, nor the costumes—there are neither—but this 140-person village in the shadow of Château de Biron holds the quintessential French experience—at least in our minds. The party takes place every year, a few days before Bastille Day (July 14). The first year we went, we stayed at the historic inn, Le Prieuré, in the heart of the village and owned by our now dear friend Sally Evans. The five-hundred-year-old priory is rumored to have a passageway beneath its ancient floors, leading directly to the château. We have yet to uncover the secret door, but we do feel as if we've uncovered one of the Dordogne's best-kept secrets.

Biron's fête is intimate, and that's what really struck us. It is off the beaten path enough to deter the tour buses, and yet has all the friendliness of a neighborhood party where new friends are welcomed.

When we arrived the first time, people actually approached us, shook our hands, and gave Sally the usual kiss-kiss on the cheeks. With only a couple hundred attendees at most, we actually had a chance to meet locals and experience a real village gathering, something pretty rare these days.

Each year in Biron, two long communal tables are set up on the main (only) Place Jean Poussou, with the castle as the regal backdrop. The meal preparation is an event in itself, with villagers cooking all day just behind Le Prieuré. The first year we watched as a group of about five men cooked ducks that turned all day on an unusual merry-go-round–like spit. Two years ago, the organizers were a little short staffed, so we pitched in to help cook and serve the meals. When we arrived this year, we tried to pay for our dinners and were refused, the coordinators insisting instead that we be their guests in thanks for our help last year. It is incredible that they remembered us, but that's the beauty of Biron.

The meal is hand delivered one by one along the tables by an army of volunteers, and BYOB applies. Beware of the home-brewed punch and giant ladle, unless you are lucky enough to be staying only thirty staggering steps away, like we do. A DJ is set up under the *halle,* and after dinner with Sally and some new friends from a neighboring village, the rhythmic sounds get us on our feet. A brief pause for some polka music is a tad confusing, but there are some takers. We reload on the punch and admire the moves. Fireworks over the majestic castle crown the euphoric evening, and as we gather to watch, we hear a lot more foreigners in Biron tonight than in years past.

Perhaps our secret is out, but that's okay. There is plenty of party to go around in the Dordogne. After a few more ladlefuls of the punch, we say, the more the merrier!

Handmade flowers dangle above the Félibrée.

-·» BRIGITTE'S BIRON «·-

WHEN YOU COME FROM big cities like we do, you can't help but imagine what it must be like to grow up in a place like Biron, where everyone knows everyone else, and you can cross the town (on foot) in thirty seconds. Despite its *petit* size, Biron has a grand history. The château, the site of one of Périgord's four baronies (the other three were Beynac, Mareuil, and Bourdeilles), is a classified historic monument. The Gontaut-Biron family owned the castle for eight centuries, but it now belongs to the department of the Dordogne.

We met Brigitte Poussou at the Le Prieuré, Biron's only inn and the former castle priory. The beautiful brunette was married in the only church and has lived in the village for more than thirty years. Her surname even graces the town square since her father-in-law, Jean Poussou, was Biron's mayor for twenty-five years. It was he who started the annual fête, a fact commemorated by a plaque in the square, and Brigitte's mother-in-law once ran the village's lone restaurant. When Brigitte refers to Biron, she says, "my village," and places her hand on her heart, a gesture we find touching. "A lot has changed since I first moved here, but the family ties are still here," Brigitte says.

In a town that could fit inside a small American shopping mall, it doesn't seem that much could change. But according to Brigitte, Biron has seen a renaissance of sorts, with old buildings now restored and the castle going from private to public ownership in 1978. Once in total ruins, the massive château, which was cobbled together in various architectural styles, has been transformed into a well-preserved tribute to the region's history and is now a tourist stop with impeccable views. Despite all the change, Brigitte says the quality of life and the friendly people of Biron still remain.

As is the case in most households in the Dordogne, food takes center stage in Brigitte's home. When we ask her about local culinary traditions, Brigitte tells us her husband and son like to *faire chabrol*, the Périgord custom of splashing wine in the bottom of the soup bowl and drinking it. "I don't like that," she laughs.

She also reveals her recipe for a real Périgord specialty, *la mique*, something we had never heard of before. But ask any native of the Dordogne if he knows about it, and he responds, "*Mais bien sur*!" But, of course! After many hand signals and consultations in our French guides, we finally guessed *la mique* was like a meatball? Wrong. More French, some sign language, and many laughs later, here is what we can tell you: it's not bread and it's not quite a dumpling or a meatball. It's simply *la mique*!

We walked with Brigitte through "her village" and watched her disappear at the point where the road dipped down below the castle and took her back to family. It is clear the village belongs to Brigitte. But as Biron was our home away from home for many years, we say, with our hands over our own hearts, it will always be a little bit ours too. ∎

❧ THE NEXT ACT ❧

"It was like being at the theater."

AFTER MANY SUMMERS spent in the hills and valleys of the Dordogne, we recognize that around every corner lives the spirit of celebration that is a part of life here, and it's precisely this spirit that we encountered when we crossed over the Lot River and turned right down an unmarked lane in the village of Touzac.

On the day we arrived at La Source Bleue, a wedding had just taken place on the sprawling lawn along the riverbank, in a sanctuary set among bamboo trees and gardens. Virginie Bouyou is accustomed to playing hostess at weddings and impromptu parties at her family compound, which comprises a bed-and-breakfast called La Tour run by Virginie and her husband, Rutger; a hotel operated by her brother, Jean-Pierre; and the restaurant La Source Enchantée. While the complex now draws travelers, fine diners, and wedding guests, it was once the home of Comédie-Francaise actress Marguerite Moreno. She was the cousin of Virginie's father, Pierre, and like an aunt to Virginie. Their home became a country retreat for Parisian bohemians of the 1920s and 1930s.

Among the well-known guests who have dined and danced on these hallowed grounds is Colette, the celebrated and controversial French author of more than fifty books. She is perhaps best known in the United States for her novel *Gigi*, which was later adapted to the stage. Colette also penned dozens of letters to her best friend, Marguerite Moreno, as documented in her book *Lettres à Marguerite Moreno*. Symbolist writer Marcel Schwob, who was married to Marguerite Moreno for five years, also spent time here.

Up until three years ago, La Tour was still the Bouyou family home. Virginie, her brother, and her father were all born here. Virginie's eyes glisten as she remembers sneaking downstairs as a young girl and peering through the banister rails. "It was like being at the theater," she recalls.

Virginie's mother, Micheline, age one hundred, also remembers the cultivated and bohemian evenings, and her own cooking. Virginie laughs at her mother's memory. Virginie remembers it slightly differently: "There were four chefs in the kitchen doing all the cooking, and it wasn't until age forty-five that my mother cooked! Food was scarce at La Source Bleue and meals were important. Almost everything was produced or grown on the property." We asked Virginie how the family supported itself. "We did nothing," she says. "My dad was a gentleman farmer and an actor. We sold our wine to La Coupole in Paris. He enjoyed life in the country but often took his plane to Paris to perform with Marguerite Moreno."

The property wasn't always a residence. It was once a working paper mill, and three water-fueled mills dating back to the eleventh and fifteenth centuries are still standing. A stroll around the place reveals peaceful nooks and crannies that would appeal to anyone looking to escape for a weekend wedding, or a lifetime. A small, covered terrace looks as if it holds a few secrets too, and we wonder who climbed the private stairs that lead to Marguerite Moreno's former quarters, and who crept home when the music faded.

The ancient house is a museum, with old photos, memorabilia, and paintings covering every square inch. We have always wanted to visit Paris in the days when Ernest Hemingway, Colette, Anaïs Nin, and Henry Miller were scribing their magnificent prose. And we have always wondered where these denizens of pleasure went to escape,

unwind, and party. Now we know. We can almost smell the stale cigarette smoke and hear the Victrola's tinny cry. If ever walls could talk, this would be a most auspicious time.

The upstairs rooms of La Tour are now guest rooms. Each floor has a common area crammed with inviting chairs and books. "We don't have a guest house to make money," Virginie says. "We simply do it to keep things up and to meet people."

Downstairs is the suite of rooms that were once Marguerite Moreno's private quarters. The room where she slept is still as it was when the actress lived here, with two twin beds and a mirror in the bathroom befitting a Hollywood dressing room. Hung above the dresser is a recognizable image of Marguerite Moreno in white makeup with black circles around her eyes as she appeared in the play *La Folle de Chaillot* (*The Madwoman of Chaillot*). "She was a kindred spirit with poets and artists," reflects Virginie. "She was dramatic and tall, and she had an impact on anyone who met her."

Marguerite Moreno died here in 1948, but her free-spirited life is palpable in the air around us, in the paintings, in her family, and in the guests who continue to be lured here to celebrate and to escape. "It begins again," says Virginie. "Actors are coming again. Jean-Claude Brialy, the French actor who just died, he came here. And other artists and people from around the world—they all come, and we all understand each other."

Virginie emphasizes that La Source Bleue has always been "a gathering place," and she intends to keep it that way. We agree. It seems the perfect blend of hideaway and dance the night away.

Around the dining table, we eat some of Virginie's homemade walnut cake, her mother's recipe, and unique from others we have tried, thanks to its thick mocha icing. Rutger pours us some of his homemade walnut wine. We "*tchin-tchin*" to new friends, and Virginie takes pictures of us before we hug and kiss good-bye, and tells us she looks forward to seeing us again, as if the date has already been set.

Finding La Source Bleue all those years ago after taking a wrong turn over a bridge was a happy accident for us. Virginie maintains that it was simply the road we were meant to take—and one that will bring us back again. "This place has always attracted interesting people. I don't know why," says Virginie. "People just arrive."

We think she's right. Somehow we, like many others, were drawn by the bewitching power of La Source Bleue. Virginie walks us to our car, and a breath of wind swirls up a cloud of dust on the gravel driveway. Virginie looks back for a moment at the house and smiles. If we are not mistaken, we can just make out the music. The curtain is up, and the next act has begun ■

The house at Source Bleue where Marquerite Moreno once lived is now a bed-and-breakfast.

Brigitte's La Mique

This combination of stale bread, meat, and vegetables is one of the Dordogne's most familial dishes. *La mique*, pronounced "la meek," is a sort of dumpling that is normally the size of a softball but can also be the size of a large round of bread. Brigitte makes hers a little smaller to absorb more of the flavor from the soup stock. The stock can be a mélange of various vegetables, and you can add sausage, bacon, or ham to make it richer.

To make the stock, in a large stockpot over medium-high heat, combine the pork, ham hocks, and water. Cover and cook for 1 hour. Add the leeks, carrots, celery, turnip, and cabbage and continue to cook for 1 hour longer. Taste and adjust the seasoning with salt. If desired, remove the salt pork and cut into serving pieces and pull the meat from the ham hocks. Discard the hocks and return the meat to the pot.

To make the dumplings, place the bread cubes in large bowl and break them up with your hands or a spoon. Add 5 of the eggs and the duck fat and knead with your hands to make a large dough ball that is dense but not hard. If the bread is too hard, knead the dough as well as you can, cover with plastic wrap, and refrigerate overnight.

Add the salt, pepper, garlic, and parsley and knead until the dough is mostly smooth; add another egg, if necessary, to achieve the desired consistency. Shape the dough into 6 softball-size balls.

Bring the stock to a boil and carefully lower a dough ball into the stock. If the dough does not stick together, remove and discard the ball and roll the remaining balls in flour. Carefully lower the remaining balls, one at a time, into the stock. Reduce the heat to low, cover, and simmer for 20 minutes.

Spoon 1 dumpling into a serving bowl with some of the stock, meats, and vegetables, and serve.

MAKES 6 SERVINGS

For the stock:

1 pound (500 g) salt pork

3 large ham hocks

3 quarts (3 liters) cold water

2 cups chopped leeks (about 2 to 3)

4 carrots, peeled and chopped

3 celery stalks, chopped

1 turnip, peeled and chopped

1 medium green cabbage,
cut into large chunks

Coarse salt

For the dumplings:

6 cups (500 g) day-old Italian or
baguette bread, torn into small pieces

5 or 6 extra-large eggs

5 tablespoons (75 g) duck fat,
bacon grease, or melted butter

2 teaspoons coarse salt

1 teaspoon cracked black pepper

1 small garlic clove, minced

2 tablespoons chopped fresh parsley

Fricassée of Rabbit
with Prunes and Red Wine

Saint Hubert's Day, November 3, is the beginning of the hunting season in France. The traditional Saint Hubert's Day hunt typically begins with a mass and the blessing of a special type of bread, which is then given to the hunting dogs. Dishes are often called "à la Saint Hubert" in honor of this patron saint of the hunt and the celebration feast that follows.

———————————————◆◆———————————————

Rinse the rabbit pieces, pat dry with paper towels, and place in a large bowl. Pour half of the wine over the rabbit and add the carrot, onion, and thyme, and stir to coat. Cover and refrigerate overnight.

Place the prunes in a bowl. Pour the remaining wine over the prunes and let stand several hours, up to overnight.

Remove the rabbit pieces from the marinade, letting any excess marinade drip back into the bowl. Lightly dust the pieces with flour and season with salt and pepper. Set the rabbit aside on a plate. Strain and reserve the marinade.

Preheat the oven to 350°F (165°C).

In a large, heavy frying pan over medium heat, cook the bacon until browned, 6 to 8 minutes. Transfer the cooked bacon to a large baking dish, leaving the drippings in the pan. Add the shallots and mushrooms to the pan and season with salt and pepper. Cook until the shallots and mushrooms are browned. Transfer the vegetables to the baking dish with the bacon. Melt the butter in the pan and add the rabbit pieces. Cook the rabbit, turning to brown all sides, about 15 minutes. Add the rabbit to the baking dish.

MAKES 4 SERVINGS

1 rabbit (about 3 lb/1.5 kg),
cut into 8 pieces

1 bottle (250 fl oz/750 ml) dry red wine

1 carrot, chopped

1 small onion, chopped

1 tablespoon chopped fresh thyme

1 pound (500 g) prunes, pitted

All-purpose flour for dusting

Coarse salt and cracked pepper

¼ pound (125 g) slab bacon,
cut into pieces

6 shallots, peeled and halved

8 oz (250 g) white mushrooms,
brushed clean

3 tablespoons (43 g) unsalted butter

¼ cup (60 ml) brandy

1 cup (250 ml) beef or veal stock

Pour the brandy into the frying pan and cook for a few seconds. Add the reserved marinade, the stock, and the prunes with their liquid. Raise the heat to high and bring the mixture to a boil. Reduce the heat to medium-low and simmer for 5 minutes. Pour the sauce over the rabbit in the baking dish.

Using tongs, turn the rabbit to coat with the sauce. Place the baking dish in the oven and bake for 35 minutes. Stir the sauce and season to taste with salt and pepper. Bake until the rabbit is tender, about 15 minutes longer.

Serve with crunchy bread or oven-roasted or mashed potatoes.

Seared Foie Gras
with Fresh Raspberries and Cognac

Foie gras is always on the menu during the holidays. Whether it is prepared in terrines or seared, you can count on this Dordogne staple to make an appearance on family tables. There are dozens of ways to prepare this timeless recipe, but this is among our favorites.

Heat 1 tablespoon of the butter in a heavy skillet over high heat. Carefully place the foie gras slices in a single layer in the skillet and season with salt and pepper. Brown the slices quickly, about 1 minute on each side.

Carefully add the Cognac and swirl the pan, allowing the flames to subside. Remove the foie gras from the pan and place one slice on each serving plate.

Add the remaining butter and the walnut liquor to the pan. Stir to combine, reduce the heat slightly, and add the raspberries. Cook until heated through, then drizzle the sauce and raspberries evenly over the foie gras. Garnish with the walnuts, if desired.

MAKES 6 SERVINGS

3 tablespoons (42 g) unsalted butter, divided

8 ounces (250 g) fresh foie gras, cut into 6 slices

Coarse salt and cracked pepper to taste

3 tablespoons Cognac

2 tablespoons walnut liquor

1 ½ cups (185 g) fresh raspberries

½ cup walnuts, for garnish (optional)

Virginie's Walnut Gâteau with Mocha Glaze

MAKES 6 SERVINGS

For the cake:

1 cup (250 g) walnuts, ground

½ cup (125 g) Périgord or black walnuts, ground

2 tablespoons all-purpose flour

10 extra-large egg whites

1 cup (250 g) sugar

For the glaze:

1 tablespoon instant coffee

1 tablespoon walnut liqueur

10 extra-large egg yolks

1 cup (250 g) sugar

½ pound (250 g) unsalted butter, softened

Whole walnuts (for garnish)

Virginie's walnut cake recipe comes from her mother, but it's her husband, Rutger, who handpicks the walnuts at just the right time of year. If you can't find Périgord walnuts, you can mimic their distinct flavor by using black walnuts. The mocha glaze is what sets this cake apart from those found in markets and restaurants.

To make the cake, preheat the oven to 350°F (180°C). Butter and flour three 8-inch (20-cm) round cake pans.

In a medium bowl, stir the walnuts and the flour until combined.

In a large mixing bowl, beat the egg whites and sugar until stiff peaks form. Carefully fold half of the flour-walnut mixture into the egg whites until almost fully incorporated. Fold in the remaining flour-walnut mixture until thoroughly incorporated. Divide the batter evenly among the prepared pans. Bake until the center of each cake is just firm when touched with your fingertip, 8 to 10 minutes. Let the cakes cool completely and turn out onto a baking rack.

To make the glaze, stir the coffee into the walnut liquor until dissolved; set aside.

In a large mixing bowl, combine the egg yolks and sugar. Set the bowl over (not touching) a saucepan filled halfway with barely simmering water. With a wire whisk, beat vigorously without stopping until the egg mixture is very thick and pale yellow. Remove the bowl from the heat, stir in the coffee mixture, and let cool. Beat in the butter until smooth.

To assemble the cake, place one of the cake layers on a serving plate and, using an offset spatula, spread the top and side with the glaze. Repeat with the second and third layers. Decorate the top of the cake with whole walnuts and serve.

Fresh Berry Crêpes

MAKES 6 SERVINGS

For the crêpes:

1 cup (250 ml) whole milk

3 extra-large eggs

½ teaspoon coarse salt

1 cup (125 g) all-purpose flour

4 tablespoons (57 g) unsalted
butter, melted

Vegetable oil for crêpe pan

For the custard:

2 cups (500 ml) whole milk

2 extra-large eggs
plus 2 extra-large yolks

6 tablespoons (72 g) sugar,
plus some for garnish

6 tablespoons (37.25 g)
all-purpose flour

⅛ teaspoon coarse salt

2 tablespoons (30 g) unsalted butter

1 teaspoon (15 ml) vanilla extract

2 cups (500 ml) heavy whipping cream,
lightly whipped

2 tablespoons (30 ml) dark rum
(optional)

February 2 is the religious holiday of *La Chandeleur* (Candlemas). But because the table ordains many practices in France, February 2 is also referred to as Crêpe Day. The tradition is to hold a coin in one hand and a crêpe pan in the other, then flip the first crêpe into the air. If the crêpe lands back in the pan, luck and prosperity will follow. Our friend Roland recalls his grandmother's crêpes and her ritual of asking him to take one to the chickens in order to bring them health and lots of eggs throughout the year. "You know, the chickens would only eat half the crêpe," he revealed to us. Seeking a deeper understanding of these Périgourdine chickens, we leaned in and asked why. "Because I ate the other half on the way to the chicken coop." Share our dressed-up version with friends, family, and, if you wish, your chickens.

◆◗◆◗◆

To prepare the crêpes, process the milk, eggs, salt, flour, and butter in a blender or whisk well. Cover and refrigerate for at least 1 hour or overnight. Stir well before using. The batter should be the consistency of heavy cream. Try a test crêpe and thin with a bit of water if necessary.

Heat an 8-inch (20-cm) crêpe pan over medium heat until a drop of water sizzles. Brush or wipe the pan with a small amount of vegetable oil. Pour a small ladle of the batter in from the side of the pan and quickly swirl the pan so the bottom is coated evenly with batter.

Small bubbles will appear when the crêpe is ready to turn. Cook for only a few seconds on the second side. Slide the crêpe out of the pan and onto a plate. Continue making crêpes, stacking them as they are finished.

To prepare the custard, heat the milk in a saucepan over medium heat until small bubbles appear.

In a medium mixing bowl, beat the eggs, yolks, sugar, flour, and salt until pale yellow. Slowly add about a cup of the hot milk to the egg mixture, stirring well. Return the warm egg-milk mixture to the saucepan with the hot milk and cook over medium-low heat, stirring constantly, until the custard has thickened.

Pour the custard into a clean bowl and stir in the butter and vanilla. Cool, stirring occasionally, then chill the custard.

Spoon about ¾ cup (170 ml) of the custard into a small bowl, stir in about half of the whipped cream, and flavor with rum if desired. Set aside.

To serve, mix the berries together. Fill each crêpe with a generous spoonful of the chilled custard. Roll into a cylinder. Arrange the crêpes in heat-proof serving bowls.

Divide the berries over the crêpes. Spoon some of the rum custard sauce over each crêpe. Sprinkle with about 2 tablespoons of sugar and use a crème brûlée torch to caramelize the sugar, for about 30 seconds. Garnish with the toasted almonds.

For serving:

1 cup (125 g) fresh raspberries

1 cup (125 g) fresh blueberries

1 cup (125 g) wild strawberries

½ cup (50 g) sliced almonds, toasted, for garnish

Vin de Noix (Walnut Wine)

The aperitif of choice in the Dordogne is this sweet dark wine made from green walnuts picked between La Fête de St. Jean (June 24) and Bastille Day (July 14). Green walnuts are not a different variety, but rather immature walnuts whose hard shells have not yet formed. It's the smooth green skin and soft interior that gives the elixir its unique flavor. There are hundreds of family recipes in the Dordogne (each claiming to be the very best, of course), but most agree the longer it sits in the cupboard the better . . . and it's worth the wait! Here is the typical recipe, but we've added some suggestions so you can start your own family tradition.

Place the quartered walnuts in a large glass container. Add the red wine and sugar.

If using nutmeg, clove, vanilla bean, and zest, add them here. Be careful not to add too much spice as you don't want to overpower the wine's flavor. Cover the container tightly and store in a cool dark room or cellar. After six weeks, strain the mixture and add the brandy. Pour into bottles and seal tightly.

Let the wine rest for at least six months. Serve in small aperitif glasses before your Dordogne feast.

MAKES 8 LITRES

40 young green walnuts, quartered

5 quarts (4.74 liters) dry red wine

2 pounds (1 kg) sugar

1 teaspoon ground nutmeg (optional)

4 cloves (optional)

1 vanilla bean, split in half (optional)

Zest of 1 small mandarin orange (optional)

1 quart (1 liter) brandy

Chapter 8

The Changing of the Guard

THE native inhabitants of the Dordogne are called *Périgourdiens*, but the region is also home to many people who hail from other countries. An estimated five hundred thousand British citizens live in France full-time, and an estimated one hundred thousand of those live in and around the Dordogne. So noticeable is their presence that locals jokingly call the region "Dordogneshire." But it's not just the English who have settled here. Over the last decade, a large contingent of Dutch, Spanish, Italians, and Parisians (locals argue they are foreign too) have slowly moved in. Some residents grumble about the elevated real estate prices, and the traffic is worse now than it was ten years ago, but local farmers, hoteliers, artisans, and small businesses don't discourage the foreign settlement and tourism, as evidenced by the signs reading "English Spoken Here" affixed to many windows. For us, the foreign influence blended with old traditions has only enhanced our experience and adds to the allure of this remarkable region. Traveling is educational if you allow it to be, and we have learned many important lessons along our journey—principally that preconceived stereotypes of a region or a people should be ignored.

When we first telephoned our favorite ice cream man, Roland Manouvrier, he was a little gruff. Unfriendly is what we deduced. When we had to call a second time to tell him we'd be an hour late, we were treated in the same icy manner. Our first reaction was to forget about talking to him, but had we

Foreign influence adds an international flavor to
Dordogne's markets and kitchens.

written him off as a rude Frenchman and not persevered, we would never have met an innovative and intelligent creator and genuinely nice guy who turned into one of our closest allies and someone we now proudly call a friend. Despite his obvious pleasure at poking fun at our French, Roland also put us at ease by regarding our mistakes as "foreign charm."

Even cuisine in the Dordogne is pigeonholed. We recently read an article by British restaurant critic Jay Rayner, a well-versed food writer. Concerning the Dordogne, he wrote, "Every single restaurant in the region serves exactly the same bloody food: duck confit, foie gras, more duck confit, herb omelettes, duck confit, and more duck bloody confit." Perhaps it was just a gross exaggeration for comic effect, but we emphasize that it takes effort and desire to uncover the essence of a place. This article made us wonder if the writer had ever cooked with a local chef, tasted fresh truffles (which he doesn't even mention), witnessed the alchemistic magic in the kitchens of La Brucelière or L'Esplanade, or stepped into L'Essentiel or one of the other three Michelin-star restaurants of the Dordogne, where duck is often *not* on the menu. If he had, perhaps he would have seen beyond the cliché he criticizes; it's like saying every restaurant in the United States serves exactly the same thing: hamburgers, hot dogs, and more bloody hamburgers.

It would be great to say the welcomes are always warm, and for the most part, they are. We have rarely experienced anything but willingness to make us feel at home. But our friend Katie did recount a curious story about an interaction at the ticket window (*guichet*) at the train station. An American learning French, Katie told us her conversation went something like this (translation in parentheses):

KATIE: *Bonjour. Parlez-vous anglais?* (Hello. Do you speak English?)

GUICHET GUY: *Non.* (Maybe. Depends on who's asking.)

KATIE: *Pas de problème. Je parle un peu français.* (No problem. I speak a little French.)

Upon detecting Katie's American accent—it seems we can never hide it, no matter how hard we try—the *guichet* guy's demeanor thawed a little, but he still had one more question.

GUICHET GUY: *Vous-êtes anglaise?* (Are you English?)

KATIE: *Non, je suis americaine.* (No, I am American.)

GUICHET GUY: Oh, I speak English. (Oh, I'm a jerk and just didn't want to help a British person.)

Detour
CHÂTEAU DES MILANDES

JOSEPHINE Baker is one of Europe's most cherished entertainers, and Ernest Hemingway once called her the most beautiful woman in the world. The American-born expatriate who later became a French citizen was a singer and dancer who took Paris by storm in the 1920s. After retiring from her career in entertainment, she adopted twelve orphans of different ethnicities and nationalities whom she fondly called her "rainbow tribe" and raised them at Château des Milandes, her five-hundred-year-old castle on the Dordogne River. The chateau is now open to the public, and we visited one day, just in time to see a bird of prey show that is held on the premises each day. Falcons, owls, and even an eagle were trained to fly over and between our heads. Once inside, things were not quite as active. Still, a journey through each of the rooms told us that Madame Baker was not just a formidable and respected entertainer but a mother. Her gowns were on display, faded and tired, along with mementos and photos, letters, and medals she received over her life. Many of the rooms are as she left them, and tucked into one corner is even a Mother's Day card with the names of her twelve children scrawled inside. Josephine is rumored to have smuggled secret messages on her sheet music during World War II, and she became a heroine of the French Resistance. She lived at Château des Milandes until her death in 1975, and her memory lives on in the Dordogne. ∎

Exotic fruits are finding their way to markets.

What a disappointment to learn someone in a position to help foreign travelers, English or otherwise, would represent his country in such a negative way. But like we said, preconceived stereotypes and generalizations are not constructive, and one interaction out of thousands could not (and should not) tarnish the brilliance of a place.

Compared to ten years ago, the Dordogne's social landscape has definitely changed, but that's a good thing. Like our friend Nicolas said, "It's the people that really make the difference," and we naturally think of our own endeavor to create a book reflective of a place, beyond the clichés and stereotypes. For us, it has been all about the people too.

One of our last meals in the Dordogne was at Château Les Merles, a rapidly rising new hotel and restaurant earning the respect of locals and foreigners alike. Around our table were French, British, South African, American, and Dutch. Like a revolving door, people came and went from our table, passed around introductions to new arrivals, laughed and waved at neighbors and old-time residents, and the chefs even sent over new menu items for us to try. We felt happy and at home here, and it was at this point we realized that *this* was a picture of what the Dordogne is becoming. In our opinion, the region is even more appealing because of it.

There is no question in our minds that without the influx of divergent and distinct cultures, our Dordogne stories would be bland. It is the stock of Périgord tradition and heritage spiced up with foreign flavor and new possibility that has created the hearty stew in which our tales and recipes simmer. We hope you have enjoyed every mouthful.

⇾❧ WELCOME TO OUR NEIGHBORHOOD ❧⇽

"It's not where you come from but how you act when you get there that matters."

IN THE BASTIDE of Monpazier, Arjan and Marije Capelle have set up a home. Like other residents, they attend town meetings, send their kids to the local school, and receive friendly waves from early morning walkers in flat, wool hats. At first glance, it appears they have a Monpazier pedigree, but the Capelles arrived only five years ago from Holland to take over the historic Edward 1er Hotel. Since then they have opened two restaurants and have seamlessly fit into this medieval hamlet of 503 official residents, without struggle or regret. This is not an easy task in a village that holds history and legacy close to home, but the right blend of outlook and ambition is key to their success and to the hearts of the citizens of Monpazier. Over coffee and some sweets, we sat down with the couple in the cozy pub of their hotel.

"We were here two weeks when our neighbor told us he heard from the hairdresser that we were nice people," says Arjan, laughing. "But the funny thing is . . . we had never met the hairdresser."

Word of mouth travels fast when newcomers arrive. When Arjan and Marije first applied to rent their house, the owner, a Monpazier lifer, received calls from villagers asking if she was going to rent to "those Dutch people" and wasn't sure if she should rent it to them. Arjan says it wasn't about their being Dutch, but about their not being from the village. Eventually, the homeowner decided that Arjan and Marije were "okay people" and rented them the home they have since bought.

This sense of neighborhood pride and protectionism is something Arjan and Marije lacked in Holland, where they lived in an apartment block with six other families to whom they never spoke. Marije smiles at the difference in lifestyle and tells us her husband's morning walks to the *boulangerie* (bakery) can take up to hour because of the neighborhood chitchat. "Here, you wouldn't dare *not* talk to your neighbors," adds Arjan.

The duo left Holland seeking a better quality of life and better weather, and brought with them the right attitude. Arjan says they made sure to introduce themselves immediately around the village when they first arrived. The hotel had no restaurant on-site, and when they first told locals about plans to add a high-end restaurant, the response was less than enthusiastic. "They said, 'Are you crazy? A foreigner can't open a restaurant in this part of France.'"

Today the elegant hotel restaurant is open seasonally and is wildly successful. Marije is busy as its chef and manager, as well as running their new, more casual venture, Bistrot 2, which opened in 2007, just a stone's throw from one of Monpazier's ancient gates. "We thought it would be nice to have a local place open year-round, where you can have coffee, tea, or a good meal in a relaxed environment that is easygoing and family-friendly," she says.

In both restaurants, Marije prepares lighter versions of Périgord recipes using fresh products from the area, sometimes combining them with ingredients from elsewhere to give a new spin on an old idea. She also insists the ambiance of the restaurant be warm and appealing, and makes sure the presentation of her tables is as beautiful as the dishes she serves. We are pleased to see candles on the tables and civilized lighting, at least compared to the garish cafeteria-like glare that haunts typical French brasseries.

The Capelles say that while they have felt no resistance from the local establishment, they have been surprised by a few cultural differences. "Sunday lunch," they both agree. "It is really embedded in the culture here to have a big meal on Sunday. Coming from Holland, we were not accustomed to sitting down for a four-hour meal."

When he's not behind the reception desk at the hotel, Arjan is often serving tables at Bistro 2. We have frequented the place on many occasions, for a long dinner in winter or a summertime lunch on the terrace, and each time we noticed the eclectic mix of people the place attracts. He squeezes us in at a cozy table tonight for a piping-hot bowl of tomato soup with a few small pieces of duck hidden on the bottom. The foie gras is expertly prepared and worth trying. The restaurant is packed, and we hear a mix of French, English, and other languages we can't make out.

We ask Arjan how he thinks they have managed to fit so well into a village as historic as Monpazier. Arjan sums it up with advice we should all heed: "It's not where you come from but how you act when you get there that matters."

Arjan heads out the front door toward Monpazier's main square to pick up supplies. Of course, he doesn't make it far—he stops about ten feet from the front gate to chat with a neighbor. ■

GOING DUTCH IN THE DORDOGNE

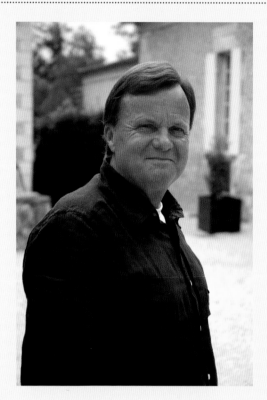

"We just created it the way we liked it, and it feels right."

WHEN JAN VAN GRINSVEN first had the idea to move to warmer climes, a small vineyard and a bed-and-breakfast in Spain had been in the forefront of his mind. Never in a million years would he have envisioned his family buying a dilapidated golf club in a small Dordogne village.

"The place was completely run-down when we bought it," Jan says with a chuckle. "The only inhabitants were animals and insects." Still, he says, something intrigued him about the place when he first saw it, and despite it not being a vineyard in Spain, he asked his family to come aboard and took the challenge head-on.

Today, Château les Merles in Tuilières is a family-run, fifteen-room luxury hotel with a casual bistro, a gourmet restaurant, and a thriving two-hundred-member golf club and spa. The family lives and works on the property; Jan's daughters, Karlijn and Judith, manage the hotel and restaurant, while Judith's husband oversees the building and golf course maintenance. Judith is also responsible for the comfortably chic decor.

When we arrive, it is a typical sunny Dordogne day, and Karlijn is pouring wine and chatting with guests. Our dining companions have called to say they are late, so Jan hands us the keys to a golf cart so we can tour the estate. Dodging golf balls and gullies, we check out the organic vegetable garden and greenhouse that provide the restaurants with fresh produce year-round.

Unlike most French restaurants that close between lunch and dinner, the two at Château les Merles are open all day, seven days a week, and cater to the public, golf club members, and hotel guests, serving anything from gourmet eight-course tasting meals to simple salads. "We aren't doing standard Périgord cuisine here because we are not from the region," explains Karlijn. "There are so many good regional restaurants around that we can't do it as well."

When conceptualizing the restaurant, the goal was to be different but still use fresh local ingredients. Jan enlisted the help of his longtime friend and well-known Dutch chef Albert Kooy. Albert now spends a couple of months every year creating the menu and cooking with the two on-site chefs, Sebastian Holten and Matthijs Geerdink. Jan jokes, "And I taste it all." He also boasts that the wine list at Château les Merles is the only one in the world specializing in the wines of Bergerac.

The terrace is between the hotel and restaurant (once a barn), and the crisp, black umbrellas are a stark and modern contrast to the ancient stone buildings and pale gravel. Inside, the gray slate floors and light-colored walls emote simplicity and elegance; red roses nestle inside the bottoms of vases, adding a splash of color. A model of a sailboat called *La Bruyère Blanche* (*White Heather*) sits by the front door. The restaurant shares the boat's name, and we ask Jan about this. Prior to buying Château les Merles, he and his wife spent ten years and more than a hundred thousand nautical miles sailing on the 120-foot yacht that the model was built after. They transported guests all over the world and brought aboard top chefs and world-class wines. "I would never be here and in this business without that experience, so the boat has to be here," says Jan, delicately touching the model.

The kitchen is the heart of the restaurant and is completely open to the dining area. Only a sitting area with two white couches and a fireplace separate the two rooms, and we see different people come and go throughout the day, eating, sipping coffee, or just resting for a while to watch the chefs in action. "For me, the kitchen is like the theater. There is tension and drama and activity. People can watch, but the chefs can also see people and watch their reactions," explains Jan. "It is the soul of the business, and I saw no reason to hide it."

top: Karlijn van Grinsven
bottom: Chef Sebastian Holten

This cozy corner is reminiscent of an old, Dutch farm-house where people sat and socialized in kitchens. At Château les Merles, it is a popular gathering spot for reading, predinner *apéritifs*, and planned activities during the winter months. "We have music books in four different languages, and we invite anyone to come in their slippers and listen to the piano, or play some music of their own," says Karlijn. "Even the staff come with their guitars and bongos."

Both Jan and Karlijn liken the setting at Château les Merles to an international club. "There are a lot of foreigners here, and we wanted a place where people of all nationalities could come and meet nice people and feel comfortable. That's exactly what we see happening now." It wasn't always so, Jan says, recalling the slow start three years ago.

"The French are very resistant to change," agrees Karlijn. "We had to approach the members carefully, try to get to know them, share some wine every day, and let them know us." Jan says he's happy to be over that hurdle and laughs (somewhat vindictively) at the memory of a Dutch friend who told Jan he'd never succeed at opening a restaurant in France because the French would never eat there. Karlijn adds, "In fact, our biggest ambassadors are our members and the local people who come here."

While dining at the restaurant with our eclectic group of friends from the region and from far-flung places, it was the French man who remarked first. Admiring the open kitchen and the lively movement of people around the restaurant, he said, "This is not at all French, but it's something great."

With family aboard, a great adventure behind him, and a new one at full throttle, Jan says things have fallen nicely into place for him in the Dordogne, "Maybe because we don't come from the area, no one ever told us all our lives we should be doing things one way or another."

"We just created it the way we liked it, and it feels right," adds Karlijn.

After a sumptuous meal, we move to the couches in front of the fire and watch the young, energetic chefs on their stage. It feels right to us too. ▪

Foreign influence and spice have found a place in the Dordogne.

Mussels with Shallots, Pernod, and Saffron

The influx of foreign flavor to the Dordogne can be seen in its markets and menus. At the Sarlat market, the smell of steamed mussels in a savory broth of garlic and wine rivals the smell of duck fat. Be sure to serve these mussels with crusty baguettes for sopping up the broth.

◆▮◆▮◆

Place the mussels in the sink and run cold water over them to remove any sand. With your fingers, remove any stringy fibers attached to the shells. Discard any opened or cracked mussels.

In a large stockpot over medium heat, melt the butter. Add the garlic, shallots, and saffron and cook until fragrant, about 2 minutes. Add the tomatoes, wine, Pernod, and white pepper and bring to a full boil for 2 minutes.

Add the mussels, cover, and cook, stirring occasionally, until most of the mussels have opened, about 5 minutes. Add the tarragon and cook until all of the mussels have opened, about 1 minute longer.

Divide the mussels among large soup bowls and ladle the broth over the top. Serve with crusty baguettes.

MAKES 4 SERVINGS

8 pounds (4 kg) fresh mussels

¼ pound (125 g) unsalted butter

3 cloves garlic, minced

4 shallots, minced

¼ teaspoon saffron threads, crushed

2 medium tomatoes, chopped

1 cup (250 ml) dry white wine

⅓ cup (80 ml) Pernod

1 teaspoon white pepper

1 tablespoon chopped fresh tarragon

Château les Merles
Salt-Crusted Chicken and Sautéed Chicory with Morel Sauce

MAKES 4 SERVINGS

For the chicken:

1 whole chicken (about 3 lb/1.5 kg)

4 cups (500 g) all-purpose flour

1 cup (250 g) sea salt

1 extra-large egg, lightly beaten

1 tablespoon minced fresh thyme

Zest of 1 lemon

For the sauce:

¾ pound (375 g) dried morel mushrooms

1 cup (250 ml) Madeira wine or dry sherry

4 tablespoons (60 g) unsalted butter

¼ cup (30 g) all-purpose flour

2 cups (500 ml) chicken stock

2 cups (500 ml) heavy whipping cream

Coarse salt and cracked pepper

For the chicory:

4 heads chicory or Belgian endive

4 tablespoons (60 g) unsalted butter

½ cup (125 ml) beer

Coarse salt and cracked pepper

Sugar as needed

This recipe comes from the outstanding and creative kitchen team at Château les Merles, who often pull ingredients from their own garden right on the premises. From the impressive young chefs to the warm family that runs the estate, Château les Merles is not just dining . . . it's an experience.

———————————•❈•———————————

Preheat the oven to 425°F (220°C).

To make the chicken, rinse the chicken and pat dry with paper towels. Combine the flour, sea salt, egg, thyme, and lemon zest with enough water to make a soft dough. Lightly roll out the dough to a 12 × 16-inch (30 × 40-cm) rectangle about 1 inch (2.5 cm) thick. Place the chicken in the middle of the dough and wrap the dough completely around it. Bake the chicken, uncovered, until the dough becomes a hard crust and a thermometer inserted into the thickest part of the thigh registers 180°F (82°C), about 1 hour. Let the chicken rest for 15 minutes.

To make the sauce, place the mushrooms in a small bowl and pour the wine over them. Let the mushrooms soak for about 15 minutes.

In a saucepan over medium heat, melt the butter. Stir in the flour and cook for about 1 minute. Stir in the stock and cream. Raise the heat to medium high and bring to a low boil. Reduce the heat to a simmer and stir until the sauce is smooth, 10 to 12 minutes.

Strain the mushrooms, reserving the wine. Add the reserved wine to the sauce and cook until the sauce is reduced by one third, about 10 minutes. Add the mushrooms and season with salt and pepper. Keep warm.

Trim the any dead leaves from the chicory heads. Halve the heads and dust lightly with flour. In a heavy frying pan over medium-high heat, melt the butter. Add the chicory and sauté until almost soft, about 10 minutes. Add the beer and cook until it is reduced by half, about 8 minutes. Season with salt and pepper. Taste the chicory and add a little sugar if it tastes bitter.

Crack the salt crust off the chicken and carve the chicken. Spoon some of the chicory onto the center of each serving plate. Arrange some of the chicken on top of the chicory and ladle the sauce on top. Spoon a few mushrooms around the chicken and serve.

Grilled Duck Brochettes with Mango Sauce

Fusing unusual flavors while taking advantage of the region's natural bounty is all the rage in the modern Dordogne kitchen. The palate of products available from around the world inspired us to pair the traditional duck with the sweetness of ripe mango and the zing of Asian spices to create an entrée worthy of your next international lunch or dinner

—◆◆—

To prepare the duck, if using bamboo skewers, soak in cold water for 1 hour.

Trim excess fat from the duck breast and cut into 1½-inch (3.8-cm) cubes; set aside.

To make the marinade, combine the honey, chili sauce, five-spice powder, ginger, vinegar, soy sauce, and salt in a bowl. Add the duck to the marinade and chill for 2 to 4 hours.

To make the mango sauce, purée the mango cubes in a food processor, then place into a medium bowl. Cut the vanilla bean in half and scrape the seeds into the mango purée (reserve the pod for another use). Stir in the lime zest, lime juice, sherry, and olive oil and mix well. Chill until ready to serve.

Preheat a charcoal or gas grill to medium high. Remove the duck from the marinade and set on paper towel to remove some of the liquid. Thread the duck pieces on the skewers, using about 4 to 5 pieces for each skewer and allowing for 2 skewers per person.

Sprinkle the duck lightly with salt and pepper before arranging on the grill. Grill for 3 to 4 minutes on each side, turning often and reducing the heat if necessary.

To serve, spoon about ¼ cup (60 ml) mango sauce onto individual serving plates. Arrange the duck skewers on each plate, one crossing the other, and garnish, if desired, with mâche or cilantro leaves and sprinkle with sesame seeds.

MAKES 4 SERVINGS

For the duck:

8 bamboo or metal skewers

2 duck breasts, approximately ½ pound (230 g) each

Coarse salt and cracked pepper

For the duck marinade:

¼ cup (60 ml) honey

1 tablespoon chili sauce

1 teaspoon five-spice powder

1 teaspoon minced ginger

2 tablespoons (30 ml) balsamic vinegar

2 tablespoons (30 ml) soy sauce

½ teaspoon salt

For the mango sauce:

2 ripe mangos, peeled and cubed

1 vanilla bean

1 teaspoon lime zest

Juice of 1 small lime

1 tablespoon sherry

2 tablespoons olive oil

Mâche or cilantro leaves, for garnish (optional)

Black sesame seeds, for garnish (optional)

Marije's Truffes du Périgord

Many restaurants in France serve a bite-size sweet with coffee or tea at the end of the meal. We find this so civilized. These *mignardises*, as they are called, come from the Old French word *mignard*, which means "pretty," "graceful," or "precious." It's appropriate, then, that we received this precious recipe from the lovely Marije, and like her, these *mignardises* are irresistible. Here is Marije's tribute to the famous truffles of the region, and the small sweets that make having coffee a quintessential part of any French meal.

——————————————•●•——————————————

Place the milk chocolate, bittersweet chocolate, butter, sugar, and cream in the top of a double boiler over medium heat and slowly melt, stirring occasionally. Remove from the heat and continue to stir until the chocolate is smooth. Stir in the Armagnac and egg yolks until well combined. Pour the chocolate into a clean bowl and chill at least 12 hours.

When firm enough to roll, shape the chocolate into small balls using a melon baller or by hand, and roll in the cocoa powder. Serve in mini paper muffin cups with coffee. Truffles can be kept in the refrigerator for several days.

MAKES ABOUT 35 TRUFFLES

7 ounces (200 g) milk chocolate

2 ounces (50 g) bittersweet chocolate

2 tablespoons (50 g) unsalted butter

2 tablespoons (50 g) sugar

6 tablespoons plus (89 ml) 2 teaspoons (10 ml) heavy whipping cream

2 tablespoons (30 ml) Armagnac

2 egg yolks

1 cup (110 g) unsweetened cocoa powder

Chocolate Torte with Summer Raspberries and Chocolate Ganache

Raspberries are the perfect complement to dark chocolate. No matter who comes and goes, this decadent torte never goes out of style.

———————————◆◆◆———————————

MAKES 8 SERVINGS

For the torte:

½ pound (250 g) unsalted butter

1⅔ cups (405 g) sugar

4½ cups (400 g) good-quality unsweetened cocoa powder

5 extra-large eggs

¼ cup (30 g) all-purpose flour

¼ teaspoon coarse salt

For the filling:

2 tablespoons raspberry jam

1 tablespoon (15 ml) raspberry liqueur

1 pint (250 g) fresh raspberries, divided

For the ganache:

12 oz (350 g) semisweet chocolate, chopped

½ cup (125 ml) heavy whipping cream

Whipped cream (for garnish)

Whole raspberries (for garnish)

Preheat the oven to 300°F (150°C). Butter and flour an 11 × 17-inch (28 × 43-cm) half-sheet or jelly-roll pan.

To make the torte, in a double boiler over low heat, combine the butter, sugar, and cocoa and heat until the mixture is smooth and the sugar is dissolved. Add the eggs, one at a time, stirring after each addition. Gently stir in the flour and salt. Pour the batter into the prepared pan.

Bake just until firm to the touch, 20 to 25 minutes. Pierce any air pockets or bubbles that may have formed and let the cake cool in the pan for 15 minutes. Carefully invert the cake onto a cutting surface.

To make the filling, in a small mixing bowl, stir the raspberry jam and liqueur until smooth. Add 1½ cups (185 g) of the raspberries and mash lightly with a fork.

To assemble the cake, using a serrated knife, cut the cake lengthwise into three rectangular layers. Cover a clean sheet pan with a large piece of plastic wrap, overlapping each side by 6 inches (15 cm). Using two spatulas if necessary, carefully transfer one layer of the cake to the plastic-lined sheet pan. Spread half of the raspberry filling on top. Place the second cake layer on top of the filling, and then spread with the remaining filling. Top with the remaining cake layer. Pull the plastic wrap up on all sides of the cake and twist the ends together on top to seal the cake. Refrigerate for at least 1 hour.

To make the ganache, place the chocolate in a medium bowl. In a small saucepan over medium-high heat, warm the cream until small bubbles appear on the surface. Pour the cream over the chocolate, cover with plastic wrap, and let stand for 15 minutes. Remove the plastic wrap and stir together until the ganache is smooth.

Unwrap the cake and place on a cooling rack. Using an icing spatula, spread the top and sides of the cake with the chocolate ganache. Reserve a small amount of the ganache for drizzling. Fit a small pastry bag with a plain narrow tip and squeeze the remaining ganache in a crisscross pattern over the finished cake. Refrigerate for at least 1 hour.

To serve, cut the cake into 1½-inch (4-cm) slices. Garnish each slice with a dollop of whipped cream and a few raspberries.

Périgord Pantry

———◆———

With fresh meat, produce, and these select items in your pantry,
you'll be prepared to eat Dordogne-style anytime.

BASICS

Armagnac

Duck (goose fat)

Duck confit (canned)

Garlic

Meat stock

Morel mushrooms (dried)

Olive oil

Porcini mushrooms (dried)

Prunes

Smoked duck breast

Sweet white wine

Truffles

Truffle oil

Walnut mustard

Walnut oil

Walnuts

Walnut vinegar

Walnut wine (vin de noix)

❈ SPECIALTY FOODS ONLINE ❈

Stocking up on Dordogne's specialties has never been easier. Try these online suppliers to start a Périgord pantry of your own.

D'Artagnan

www.dartagnan.com

Foie gras, seasonal wild mushrooms, game, and poultry.

Dordogne Direct

www.dddirect.co.uk

Oils, pâtés, and regional products.

iGourmet

www.igourmet.com/frenchfood.asp

Selection of French foods, products, and recipes.

Gourmet Food Store

www.gourmetfoodstore.com/truffles

Wide selection of truffles, sauces, condiments, and duck.

D'un Terroir a l'Autre

www.dunterroir-alautre.fr

Fine organic walnut products from the Dordogne.

French Flavour

www.frenchflavour.co.uk

Roasted garlic, duck fat, sea salt, and other pantry basics.

Resource Guide

―――――◦――――――

We have included here a list of places to stay, eat, and visit, and
activities for the whole family in the Dordogne. This is by no means a
comprehensive list, and we apologize if we have left anyone out.

GETTING THERE

The Dordogne is easy to get to by plane, train, or car.

PLANE
The airports at Bergerac and Bordeaux welcome daily flights from England,
Brussels, and Paris: www.bergerac-airport.net.

TRAIN
The high-speed TGV train has more than twenty daily trips from Paris
to nearby Bordeaux: www.tgv.com and www.sncf.fr.

CAR
The main highways to the area are the A20, A10, and A89.
There are rental car agencies at the airports and at the TGV station in Bordeaux.

❧❈ PLANNING ❈❧

There are many Web sites about the Dordogne, but here are a few that offer a good slice of everything concerning the region.

www.sites-en-perigord.com

www.pays-des-bastides.com

www.pays-de-bergerac.com

Saint Front Cathedral in Périgueux

☙ LODGING ❧

From the high-end hotels and golf clubs to the family-run chambre d'hôtel and fermes auberges, there is a place to stay in the Dordogne for every budget.

Au Château
P.O. Box 26098
San Diego, CA 92196
www.au-chateau.com
info@au-chateau.com

Château Lalinde
1, rue de Verdun
24150 Lalinde
www.chateaulalinde.com
+33 (0)5 53 22 80 94

Hotel Le Forêt
2 Place Victor Hugo
24150 Lalinde
+33 (0)5 53 27 98 30

Château Les Merles
Tuilières
24520 Mouleydier
www.lesmerles.com
+33 (0)5 53 63 13 42

Château des Vigiers
24240 Monestier
www.vigiers.com
+33 (0)5 53 61 50 00

Hotel Edward 1er
5, rue Saint Pierre
24540 Monpazier
www.hoteledward1er.com
+33 (0)5 53 22 44 00

Hotel Source Bleue
Moulin de Leygues
46700 Touzac
www.sourcebleue.com
+33 (0)5 65 36 52 01

La Tour de Cause
Pont de Cause
24250 Castelnaud – La Chapelle
www.latourdecause.com
+33 (0)5 53 30 30 51

L'Esplanade
24250 Domme
www.esplanade-perigord.com
+33 (0)5 53 28 31 41

Le Prieuré au Château de Biron
24540 Biron
www.leprieurebiron.com
+ 33 (0)9 60 47 46 07

Logis de la Vignolle
24290 Saint-Amand-de-Coly
www.logis-de-la-vignolle.com
+33 (0)5 53 51 60 48

❧ RESTAURANTS ☙

It is truly impossible to name every worthwhile restaurant in Dordogne, as they are as ubiquitous as the stunning vistas. From Michelin stars to farmhouse inns, there is something to tempt every taste. Many of the hotels mentioned above also have superb restaurants.

Bistrot 2
Foirail Nord
24540 Monpazier
www.bistrot2.fr
+33 (0)5 53 22 60 64

Au Fil de l'Eau
3 Rue de la Rouquette
33220 Port Sainte Foy et
Ponchapt
+33 (0)5 53 24 72 60

**Restaurant de la
Poste**
Le Bourg
24290 Saint-Léon sur
Vézère
+33 (0)5 53 50 73 08

La Brucelière
Place de la Capelle
24560 Issigeac
www.bruceliere.com
+33 (0)5 53 73 89 61

Restaurant L'Essentiel
8 Rue de la Clarté
24000 Perigieux
www.restaurantlessentiel.com
+33 (0)5 53 35 15 15

**Ferme Auberge
D'Imbes**
La Gratadie 24590
Archignac
+33 (0)5 53 28 95 50

Le P'tit Loup
20 Rue Gabriel Peri
24150 Lalinde
+33 (0)5 53 24 90 75

Restaurant de l'Abbaye
Place Abbaye
24480 Cadouin
+33 (0)5 53 63 40 93

Ferme Auberge Maraval
24250 Cénac et St julien
+33 (0)5 53 30 26 95

WINE TASTING

Great wines and their producers are prolific in the region, numbering in the hundreds. Around Bergerac, follow the Route des Vins for a great sampling. A map is available from most tourist offices in the region.

Château de Monbazillac

Route de Mont-de-Marsan

24240 Monbazillac

www.chateau-monbazillac.com

+33 (0)5 53 63 65 00

Across the moat and through the vines, this fully furnished château and tasting room are open for visits.

Domaine du Haut Pécharmant

24100 Bergerac

www.haut-pecharmant.com

+33 (0)5 53 57 29 50

The small, off-the-beaten-path winery run by the Roches family will surely inspire you.

Château de Tiregand

24100 Creysse

www.chateau-de-tiregand.com

+33 (0)5 53 23 21 08

Tour the cellars and be royally taken by the charm and the wine of the Saint Exupéry family.

Vignobles Lajonie

Bellevue

24240 Monbazillac

www.vignobleslajonie.com

+33 (0)5 53 57 17 96

This father-and-sons operation spreads over three separate wineries: Château Pintouquet, Château Bellevue, and Château les Merles.

✂ FUN FOR FOODIES ✂

Open-air markets (see chapter 2) are a great way to taste and sample local products and meet the people who produce them. There are hundreds of local farms, shops, and ateliers to visit, often with signs on the main roads to lead the way. Cooking classes and culinary tours are also delicious ways to experience the Dordogne.

La Boire d'Imbert
46500 Rocamadour
www.rocamadourlaboriedimbert.com
+33 (0)5 65 33 20 37

*This goat farm, dairy, and cheesemaking factory is
en route to the stunning village of Rocamadour
and has a vegetable garden, baby animals, and shows
for children during the summer.*

La Borderie
24120 Chavagnac
www.cooking-truffles.com
+33 (0)5 53 51 00 24

*Visit Danièle Mazet-Delpeuch at her ancient family farmhouse
and learn the art of cooking truffles and foie gras.*

Louis Roque Distillery
46200 Souillac
www.lavieilleprune.com
+33 (0)5 65 32 78 16

*Homemade brandy has been distilled here for
generations, including the well-known LaVieille Noix.*

Le Vieux Logis
24510 Trémolat
+33 (0)5 53 22 80 06
www.vieux-logis.com

*Chef Vincent Arnould offers morning lessons, followed
by lunch in his gastronomic kitchen in Trémolat.*

Vagabond Gourmet
www.vagabondgourmet.com
+1 813.835.8348

*Chef Laura's own culinary tour company will lead
foodies to the Dordogne's best-kept secrets.*

Château Monplaisir
24240 Gageac et Rouillac
Dordogne, France
+33 (0)5 53 23 93 92
www.wineschoolbergerac.fr

*Wine writer, accredited WSET tutor, and
author Helen Gillespie-Peck teaches
full-day, weekend, and weeklong courses
from her Bergerac vineyard.*

Moulin de la Tour

24200 Sainte Nathalène

www.moulindelatour.com

+33 (0)5 53 59 22 08

*Owner Jean Pierre will lead you on a scented tour of
this sixteenth-century walnut mill, which is powered
entirely by water. After the tour, sample walnut-flavored
cakes, liqueurs, mustards, candies, and oils.*

Truffière Bressac

24510 Sainte Foy de Longas

Dordogne, France

http://truffiere.bressac.free.fr

+33 (0)5 53 22 72 39

*Huges Martin and his mutt, Mickey, will show
you around his small truffle farm near
the famous truffle market in Saint-Alvère.*

Le Bouyssou

24200 Carsac-Aillac

+33 (0)5 53 31 12 31

E-mail: elevage.bouyssou@wanadoo.fr

*Free-range geese are raised on this idyllic farm, by Nathalie
and Denis Mazet, for the production of foie gras.*

CHÂTEAUX AND GARDENS

There are more than a thousand castles to visit in this fairy-tale setting, more per square mile than in any other region of France. Many have exquisite gardens to stroll. One could (and should) explore them all, walking through centuries of history and architectural styles in quaint, pristine villages and countrysides.

Château de Beynac

24220 Beynac et Cazenac

+33 (0)5 53 29 50 40

Looming over a sheer cliff wall, crenellated walls,and double moats, Château de Beynac was an imposing fortress during the Hundred Years' War. Thankfully, it is more welcoming to visitors today.

Château de Biron

24540 Biron

+33 (0)5 53 35 50 10

Owned by the same family for eight centuries, the building has been enlarged and transformed many times, and the different architectural styles are clearly visible. Many of the rooms, including a torture chamber, are staged to give a sense of the period.

Château de Castelnaud

24250 Castelnaud-La-Chapelle

www.castelnaud.com

+33 (0)5 53 31 30 00

Facing its onetime rival Beynac across the Dordogne River, Château de Castelnaud has been picturesquely restored and now stands in peaceful harmony with its neighbors.

Château de Hautefort

24390 Hautefort

www.chateau-hautefort.com

+33 (0)5 53 50 51 23

With its classic architectural style and terraced formal gardens, this castle is reminiscent of the Loire Valley châteaux. Situated above the Auvézère Valley and Hautefort village, the renovated château houses seventeenth-century paintings.

Château des Milandes

24250 Castelnaud la Chapelle

www.milandes.com

+33 (0)5 53 59 31 21

Built in 1489, Château des Milandes fell into ruin and was later restored by the legendary American cabaret singer Josephine Baker. In addition to memorabilia, the castle has a falconry housing birds of prey, including an American bald eagle.

Château et Parc Botanique de Neuvic

R.N. 89

24190 Neuvic-sur-l'Isle

www.chateau-parc-neuvic.com

+33 (0)5 53 80 86 65

Only ten minutes from Périgueux, this riverside, sixteenth-century castle is surrounded by botanical gardens with a variety of trees, shrubs, and flowers from around the world.

Les Jardins de Manoir d'Eyrignac

24590 Salignac

www.eyrignac.com

+33 (0)5 53 28 99 71

*Among the most beautiful in France, these sculpted
English- and Italian-inspired gardens have been in
the same family for twenty-two generations
over the last five hundred years. Two restaurants and
a gift shop are located on site.*

Les Jardins Suspendus de Marqueyssac

24220 Vézac

www.marqueyssac.com

+33 (0)5 53 31 36 36

*The gardens of Marqueyssac have hiking trails,
picnic sites, and the best panoramas over the valley.
There is a restaurant on site, as well as a gift
shop, and the gardens offer organized children's
activities in the summer.*

MUSEUMS

There's always something to do and see in the Dordogne, including a wide variety of museums to visit. These unique museums promise to delight adults and captivate even the most fidgety kids.

Musée de la Guerre au Moyen Age

Château de Castelnaud
24250 Castelnaud-La-Chapelle
www.castelnaud.com
+33 (0)5 53 31 30 00

The museum at this historical monument boasts a comprehensive collection of weapons and devices that will send shivers up your spine. Boys of all ages will enjoy a visit.

Musée Nationale de Préhistoire

24620 Les Eyzies-de-Tayac
www.musee-prehistoire-eyzies.fr
+33 (0)5 53 06 45 65

This museum is a must for anyone interested in tracing the history of mankind and understanding its significance to the Dordogne. Lots of bones and life-size skeletons make this an interesting and educational outing.

Musée Atelier du Trompe l'Oeil et du Décor Peint

5 Rue Emile Combes
24000 Périgueux
www.museedutrompeloeil.com
+33 (0)5 53 09 84 40

An enchanted world of illusion unfolds before your eyes in this museum and workshop. Guided tours and beginners' courses are available; a tearoom and bookshop are on site.

❧ CAVES AND GROTTOES ❧

Existence of ancient man can be traced back twenty thousand years in the Dordogne, and the cliffs and hills of the region are riddled with mementos of prehistoric life. Here are some of the most famous.

Lascaux II

24290 Montignac

www.culture.gouv.fr/culture/arcnat/lascaux/en

+33 (0)5 53 05 65 65

This complex of caves near the village of Montignac contains paintings estimated to be sixteen thousand years old. The original caves are closed to the public, but painted facsimiles reproduce them down to the minutest details.

Gouffre de Proumeyssac

24260 Le Bugue

www.perigord.com/proumeyssac

+33 (0)5 53 07 27 47

The largest developed cavern in the Périgord, Le Bugue's underground cathedral has crystal formations that hang 150 feet from the ceiling and seem to defy gravity. Descend in a basket, like the first explorers did, or walk down with a guide.

A view from inside the Gouffre de Proumeyssac

·❈· ABBEYS ·❈·

Religion was an important aspect of daily life in the Dordogne during the Middle Ages, as evidenced by the region's many medieval churches and monasteries. These relics of the Dordogne's sacred history should not be overlooked.

Cadouin Abbey

24150 Cadouin

+33 (0)5 53 63 36 28

A pilgrimage site for centuries, this twelfth-century monastery still attracts hordes of visitors with its peacefulcloisters and serene setting.

Echourgnac Cistercian Abbey

24410 Echourgnac

+33 (0)5 53 80 82 50

Visitors enjoy the beautiful surroundings and tranquil atmosphere of this abbey. Make sure to taste the divine walnut liqueur–soaked cheese that is prepared here.

⋟ OUTDOORS ⋞

Hot air ballooning, boat trips, and biking are among the many ways for outdoor enthusiasts to explore the region. Signs for canoe and kayak rentals are everywhere along the river roads. The flat roads of the Dordogne are perfect for biking; however, traffic is heavy in the summer. You can go on an organized tour or rent a bike and go it alone.

Apolo Cycles

31 Blvd. Victor Hugo

24100 Bergerac

www.apolo-cycles.com

+33 (0)5 53 57 73 08

Offers a range of bikes, motorcycles, and scooters for short- or long-term rental. Owners Jean-Paul and Sophie can also recommend local trails.

Gabares Norbert

Le Bourg

24250 La Roque Gageac

www.gabarres.com

+33 (0)5 53 29 40 44

Float down the Dordogne River on a replica of a gabare, the traditional boat used to carry goods down the river in the eighteenth and nineteenth centuries. Tours leave from La Roque-Gageac, a picturesque village carved out of the mountainside, and worth the trip itself.

Lalinde Mountain Bike Centre

Maison de l'Ecluse

24510 Lalinde

www.pays-debergerac.com/english/leisure/lalindemoutain-bike-centre

+33 (0)5 53 24 12 31

Bicycle rental and instruction, plus guides to miles of wooded paths.

MC Moto

4 Avenue de Selves

24200 Sarlat

www.mcmoto24.com

+33 (0)5 53 59 06 11

Rents bikes, scooters, and motorcycles with daily, weekly and monthly rates.

Périgord Dordogne Montgolfières

Le Garrit

24220 Saint Cyprien

www.perigord-dordogne-montgolfieres.com

+33 (0)5 53 29 20 56

Partick Bécheau will whisk you away on a hot air balloon ride with spectacular views for the experience of a lifetime. A final toast and return to the take-off point is included in the package.

Formulas for Metric Conversion

Ounces to grams	multiply ounces by 28.35
Pounds to grams	multiply pounds by 453.5
Cups to liters	multiply cups by .24
Fahrenheit to Centigrade	subtract 32 from Fahrenheit, multiply by five and divide by 9

Oven Temperatures

Degrees Fahrenheit	Degrees Centigrade	British Gas Marks
200°	93°	—
250°	120°	—
275°	140°	1
300°	150°	2
325°	165°	3
350°	175°	4
375°	190°	5
400°	200°	6
450°	230°	8

Metric Equivalents for Volume

U.S.		Metric
⅛ tsp.		0.6 ml
½ tsp.		2.5 ml
¾ tsp.		4.0 ml
1 tsp.		5.0 ml
1½ tsp.		7.0 ml
2 tsp.		10.0 ml
3 tsp.		15.0 ml
4 tsp.		20.0 ml
1 Tbsp.	—	15.0 ml
1½ Tbsp.	—	22.0 ml
2 Tbsp. (⅛ cup)	1 fl. oz	30.0 ml
2½ Tbsp.		37.0 ml
3 Tbsp.	—	44.0 ml
1/3 cup	—	57.0 ml
4 Tbsp. (¼ cup)	2 fl. oz	59.0 ml
5 Tbsp.	—	74.0 ml
6 Tbsp.	—	89.0 ml
8 Tbsp. (½ cup)	4 fl. oz	120.0 ml
¾ cup	6 fl. oz	178.0 ml
1 cup	8 fl. oz	237.0 ml (.24 liters)
1½ cups	—	354.0 ml
1¾ cups	—	414.0 ml
2 cups (1 pint)	16 fl. oz	473.0 ml
4 cups (1 quart)	32 fl. oz	(.95 liters)
5 cups	—	(1.183 liters)
16 cups (1 gallon)	128 fl. oz	(3.8 liters)

Metric Equivalents for Weight

U.S.	Metric
1 oz	28 g
2 oz	58 g
3 oz	85 g
4 oz (¼ lb.)	113 g
5 oz	142 g
6 oz	170 g
7 oz	199 g
8 oz (½ lb.)	227 g
10 oz	284 g
12 oz (¾ lb.)	340 g
14 oz	397 g
16 oz (1 lb.)	454 g

Metric Equivalents for Length

U.S.	Metric
¼ inch	.65 cm
½ inch	1.25 cm
1 inch	2.50 cm
2 inches	5.00 cm
3 inches	6.00 cm
4 inches	8.00 cm
5 inches	11.00 cm
6 inches	15.00 cm
7 inches	18.00 cm
8 inches	20.00 cm
9 inches	23.00 cm
12 inches	30.50 cm
15 inches	38.00 cm

Metric Equivalents for Butter

U.S.	Metric
2 tsp.	10.0 g
1 Tbsp.	15.0 g
1½ Tbsp.	22.5 g
2 Tbsp. (1 oz)	30.0 g
3 Tbsp.	45.0 g
¼ lb. (1 stick)	110.0 g
½ lb. (2 sticks)	220.0 g

Index

C

R